HIGHER EDUCATION AND REGIONAL GROWTH

About Policy Network

Policy Network is an international thinktank and research institute. Its network spans national borders across Europe and the wider world with the aim of promoting the best progressive thinking on the major social and economic challenges of the 21st century.

Our work is driven by a network of politicians, policymakers, business leaders, public service professionals, and academic researchers who work on long-term issues relating to public policy, political economy, social attitudes, governance and international affairs. This is complemented by the expertise and research excellence of Policy Network's international team.

A platform for research and ideas

- Promoting expert ideas and political analysis on the key economic, social and political challenges of our age.
- Disseminating research excellence and relevant knowledge to a wider public audience through interactive policy networks, including interdisciplinary and scholarly collaboration.
- Engaging and informing the public debate about the future of European and global progressive politics.

A network of leaders, policymakers and thinkers

- Building international policy communities comprising individuals and affiliate institutions.
- Providing meeting platforms where the politically active, and potential leaders of the future, can engage with each other across national borders and with the best thinkers who are sympathetic to their broad aims.
- Engaging in external collaboration with partners including higher education institutions, the private sector, thinktanks, charities, community organisations, and trade unions.
- Delivering an innovative events programme combining in-house seminars with large-scale public conferences designed to influence and contribute to key public debates.

www.policy-network.net

About the Samuel Lindow Foundation

The Samuel Lindow Foundation was established in 1992. The foundation's research tackles important issues in contemporary society, as identified by the foundation's trustees, and these are addressed by working with its educational partner and 'Member' – UCLan – and other collaborators. The foundation has established, with UCLan, an educational institution in West Cumbria to enable it to better conduct research and advance the education of the public.

The Samuel Lindow Foundation's charitable objectives are:

- To advance the education of the public
- To conduct research and publish the results
- To establish an educational institution
- To achieve public benefit

The foundation and the university are working together to deliver a five-year integrated programme of research, funded by the Foundation and matched by the university.

About the University of Central Lancashire Applied Policy Science Unit

The Applied Policy Science Unit (APSU) is an independent political science research unit at the University of Central Lancashire (UCLan) and based at its campus on the Westlakes Science and Technology Park, near Whitehaven in West Cumbria.

The APSU's mission is to make an original and independent contribution to policy and its implementation. This unit undertakes academic research, consultancy and dissemination in the field of political science with a special focus upon the application of current policy problems. In addition to UCLan staff involved in political science research and dissemination, the APSU also involves, as advisors, individuals who are professionally involved in politics, policy and government.

There has been a political science research unit at Westlakes for almost two decades. This UCLan unit is building upon and developing that work in governance architectures and institutions, the rescaling of policy and politics and belief and value systems. This long engagement in applied policy science at the Westlakes campus in West Cumbria has given the APSU a distinctive perspective on the role of communities in a globalised economy, and in the importance of individual perceptions and beliefs, and community-level interactions in achieving a nexus between global and local processes and optimising the untraded interdependencies between organisations.

In support of its mission, APSU's objectives are:

- To facilitate and undertake applied research into policy problems confronting public, private and social sectors
- To make an independent and original contribution in the field of applied policy and political sciences
- To combine rigorous academic enquiry with the insights of experienced policy practitioners
- To act as a catalyst for the development and implementation of policy
- To disseminate the results of research through teaching, publications, seminars and conferences

HIGHER EDUCATION AND REGIONAL GROWTH

Local Contexts and Global Challenges

Edited by
Rick Wylie

policy network

ROWMAN &
LITTLEFIELD
———— INTERNATIONAL ————

London • New York

Published by Rowman & Littlefield International Ltd
Unit A, Whitacre, 26-34 Stannary Street, London, SE11 4AB
www.rowmaninternational.com

Rowman & Littlefield International Ltd.is an affiliate of Rowman & Littlefield
4501 Forbes Boulevard, Suite 200, Lanham, Maryland 20706, USA
With additional offices in Boulder, New York, Toronto (Canada), and Plymouth (UK)
www.rowman.com

British Library Cataloguing in Publication Data

A catalogue record for this book is available from the British Library

ISBN: PB 978-1-78660-831-4
ISBN: eBook 978-1-78660-832-1

Library of Congress Cataloging-in-Publication Data

Library of Congress Control Number: 2018932512

♾™ The paper used in this publication meets the minimum requirements of
American National Standard for Information Sciences—Permanence of Paper for
Printed Library Materials, ANSI/NISO Z39.48-1992.

Printed in the United States of America

CONTENTS

ABOUT THE CONTRIBUTORS

Andrew Adonis is a Labour member of the House of Lords. He is a former schools minister, and after years at the heart of government remains a leading figure in debates on higher education. In 2012 he authored of 'Education, Education, Education: Reforming England's Schools'. He is a former secretary of state for transport, and is a former chair of the National Infrastructure Commission.

Maddalaine Ansell is chief executive of University Alliance, the mission group for modern civic universities with a professional and technical focus. She came to this role from the senior Civil Service where she worked on research, higher education and skills policy.

Graham Baldwin is the vice-chancellor of Southampton Solent University. Previously he was a deputy vice-chancellor at the University of Central Lancashire and prior to that was seconded into the Nuclear Decommissioning Authority as the National Skills Research Director. Graham is an honorary professor at Hebei University and a visiting professor at the National Association of Education Administration in Beijing. He has received a title of 'Outstanding Foreign Expert' from Hebei Province, China.

David Briggs operates as an independent consultant at the interface between universities, public sector and business following 30 years in economic development for higher education, city-regional and regional agencies.

Keith Burnley has worked in senior positions at the interface between education, society and business for over twenty years. Most recently he was CEO of the National Centre for Entrepreneurship in Education until June 2016. He is now a consultant specialising in higher education, entrepreneurial organisations and staff development.

Patrick Diamond is co-chair and research director at Policy Network. He is a lecturer in Public Policy at Queen Mary, University of London, Gwilym Gibbon fellow at Nuffield College, Oxford, and a visiting fellow at the Department of Politics at the University of Oxford. Until May 2010 he was head of policy planning in 10 Downing Street and senior policy adviser to the prime minister.

John Lonsdale is director of innovation and enterprise for the University of Central Lancashire. Following his early career at Rolls-Royce plc and National Nuclear Laboratory, John joined UCLan in 2007 and now leads on partnership and business development, business incubation, intellectual property and commercialisation of research.

Mike Thomas is vice-chancellor at the University of Central Lancashire, carries out research on leadership kindness and is co-founder of the College for Military Veterans and Emergency Services.

Rick Wylie is Samuel Lindow academic director at the University of Central Lancashire's West Cumbria campus, principal of the Samuel Lindow Foundation and executive director of the UCLan Applied Policy Science Unit.

FOREWORD

Andrew Adonis

Higher education institutions in Britain have long been cultivators of knowledge to the benefit of their regions and localities. In a richly diverse sector, many owe their conception to the needs of their local communities and industries, to further advance the learning and skillsets of individuals vital to the growth of regional and national economies. The original 'redbricks' were the pride of Victorian philanthropy in provincial England. This book offers insightful examinations into both the foundations of the modern university, as well as the role in which universities play as 'anchors' in their regions today.

This book does not, however, enter into those recent debates about universities (such as those of senior staff remuneration or tuition fees) in which I have been proud to be a leading, and at times controversial, voice. These are by no means irrelevant or isolated debates, though. Big questions about the sustainability of fees and the present funding system in general undoubtedly exist. The status quo must be challenged if universities want to sustain public support. A new settlement is imperative if universities are serious about retaining the confidence of the regions they should seek to serve. Just because universities are a great British success story, it does not mean that a culture of 'anything goes' should be allowed to become prevalent. It would be their undoing.

None of these criticisms should be seen as an attempt to undermine the basic strengths of the UK higher education sector. The UK's position in leading research – four British institutions are in the global top 10, and 28 are in the global top 200 according to QS World University Rankings 2018 – is a clear demonstration that the country's universities are brilliant. This in turn furthers Britain's already high attractiveness to world-leading researchers. But it is a situation facing two glaring challenges. One is that we must make sure Brexit does not undermine that attractiveness. The other is the country's need to get better at turning our research excellence into commercial gain. The latter is a long standing problem, but one which the recent emergence of new institutions like Innovate UK and the Catapult centres can help to tackle.

We also need to be proud of diversity in the sector. Institutions that cater for less academically top-class individuals and focus less on pure research, but offer more professional training and knowledge exchange are playing a vital role. It is this diverse mix of higher education offerings which is, whilst not yet necessarily realising its maximum potential, creating a robust sector that meets the needs of many. I am particularly proud of the achievements of the Labour governments of 1997–2010, which undertook in huge efforts to increase participation in Britain's universities. The 40 per cent target we set right at the beginning of this period has now been met. Perhaps the pinnacle of this achievement is that participation of full-time students from less privileged groups has grown strongly. It is becoming clear that some of the best examples of this success are universities with a strong regional mission.

There is legitimate room for debate about whether it was right to merge existing universities with 35 polytechnics in the early 1990s. Some good things have been lost as a result of this. We have witnessed the decline of part-time degrees (which has been notably severe since the introduction of higher tuition fees) and the near-disappearance of sandwich courses. When the system should have been strengthening the ladders from apprenticeships through further education into higher education, we appear in reality to have weakened them. This is a historic mistake which must now be corrected. Strengthening the regional role of universities is a fundamental step in bringing about a positive change in direction.

Universities need to play to regional and local economic strengths. Successful regional institutions can bolster demand for university places by providing courses that are tailored to the area's current and potential economic needs. They can be an asset in addressing problems of social mobility, and must engage more successfully with schools in deprived areas. They need to offer students who are judged to have potential, but where poor quality schools have let them down, the opportunity to raise the level of their basic skills in core subjects of English, maths and science. This is crucial for ensuring better chances of entrance and graduation in STEM subject courses. There is an increasingly desperate need to attract young people into STEM career paths – so regional universities can tackle the skills shortage question as well as a social mobility one. And whilst not all degrees in the likes of media studies are bad – I do not buy that kind of populism – the regional university needs to shift its offer to courses that offer much fuller prospects of employability and career progression.

Similarly regional universities can help extend the supply side of their regional economies by offering relevant, sector-specific skills and qualifications. They need to think about how their degree offers can contribute to the enhancement of innovative business clusters that build on regional competitive strengths. The University of Central Lancashire (UCLan), a partner in the publication of this book, has a campus at Westlakes, near Whitehaven on the Cumbrian coast, which pivots its activities and ambitions around the regional economy's key future strengths. These are namely: nuclear waste management; the development of sustainable tourism; the whole range of environmental issues that come with land management and sustainable agriculture; and promoting business development in remoter parts of the country that depend on high-quality digital networks for their business model.

Beyond this, the regional university can then develop its own research and teaching capabilities on the basis of effective knowledge exchange with the business clusters its skill training and graduate provision has helped foster. A particular enthusiasm of mine is the promotion of closer links between universities and schools on the one hand and apprenticeship training, further education and higher education on the other. Once again, UCLan offers a valuable example through the co-sponsorship of an academy at Egremont, located in one of the most deprived parts of West Cumbria – co-operation between a regionally-focused university and a local school which has proven to be a success. For this to be built upon, we need a more diverse higher education sector with post-1992 universities making concerted efforts to be distinctive in their own ways, rather than copying the traditional university model. The regional role of a university is crucial to that vision of distinctiveness.

PREFACE

Rick Wylie

This book focuses on the many ways in which universities can impact upon the development of regions and what the implications of this are for regional policy. The breadth of their regional role is often unappreciated and the influence of a university spans most sectors within a region. Through their intervention and innovation with partners in the social sector and community projects, universities can affect the lives of many members of the community via their applied research and aspiration raising activities. They create new knowledge, realise it commercially and fix it locally; as businesses in their own right they engage thousands of staff and students; and the prestige a university's presence bestows upon a city, town, region and nation is seen as important. Regions that do not have one feel denied access to the, sometimes nebulous, things a university can provide. But what actually *are* those things? Well, that is the focus of this book.

Drawing upon the experiences of practitioners and scholars, and insights from case studies of policy and institutional programmes, the contributions in this book explore the role of universities in a regional context, in particular their contribution to social and economic development. The contributions also reveal the dynamic nature of the higher education sector and the flux of institutional and governmental policies, and comment upon the emergence of new institutions which shape this key educational sector. They also reveal the nature of regions, their changing geographies and the scaling and rescaling of power relations within regions shaped by the drivers of globalisation, the scope and scale of commercial and knowledge capital and the tensions between regional development and the mobility of knowledge, skills and individuals.

INTRODUCTION

Rick Wylie

For decades, universities have been seen as assets in the economic development of regions[1]. Today they are seen as central. Embedded in global knowledge economies and rooted in places and communities, they bestow prestige upon their home region (whose name they usually adopt) and act as a pipeline for resources to transform individuals, institutions, places, communities and regions into players in global networks. Regions are reassured by their possession of a university; regions that do not have one feel disadvantaged and want one.

In a regional sense, universities' contributions centre upon fixing flows of knowledge, making places 'sticky'[2] by positioning regions as "nodes on global flows of intellectual, financial and human capital assets". But they also bestow mobility upon individual students and researchers with a university education, giving individuals the asset of mobility on those same networks of flow.

Though much of the literature on universities and regions centres on their economic impact there can be a much wider impact, as the outcomes and outputs of university research add value beyond the sphere of scholarship and the economy. Put simply, through social and policy research, universities can influence the lives of individuals in all walks of life through the valorisation of their research[3] and the application of the findings of research in policy, communities and neighbourhoods. In an era when traditional models of policy provision are being reconfigured, from care of the elderly to complex healthcare systems, universities have an enormous role to play in public sector reform. In addition, universities are also significant economic actors in their own right. During 2013–14, for example, the University Centre of Lancashire contributed £200 million to the north-west of England's economy and, with 3,290 directly employed staff, is one of the largest employers in the city of Preston.

In a context of declining government funding for research at a national level and increased competition for (in the United Kingdom) largely self-funding students, the more entrepreneurial universities have, almost out of necessity, become more regional in their attitude and core activities.

An especially important element of the university's regional role is addressing regional skills agendas[4] from recruiting and retaining students locally to courses providing a skilled workforce to address identified skills gaps within a region. In the UK, local enterprise partnerships identify skills as one of the key drivers of economic development and in Cumbria, for example, the LEP skills plan sees universities and other providers as key to addressing the skills agenda as a priority to maintain the competitiveness of the Cumbria region. Clearly, a large university provides substantial regional economic benefits in respect of the spending by the institution and by students within their region. There is, however, more to the regional role of a university than providing a skilled labour force.

But what *is* a university? In contemporary society it is, as Shore argues, 'no longer clear what universities are actually for…'[5] There is no generally accepted definition of a university which covers all of its manifestations and it is a somewhat contested concept. The idea of a university has changed substantially over the years. Writing in 1852, JH Newman, in The Idea of a University, focused upon the diffusion and extension of knowledge rather than its advancement.[6] Elite and isolated, Newman's institution was rather different from the embedded and engaged university we know today – though this ivory tower isolation is still a sometimes-held view reflected in dismissing a point as "...well, that's only of academic interest...". That said, Newman's perspective *does* highlight two key points which are especially relevant to our discussion. Firstly, the universal nature of the institution and the importance of breadth and depth in a learning experience; and, secondly, the formative role of learning and the lifelong benefit of knowledge for the individual. Both of these points are extremely relevant today.

Years later, Clark Kerr, in The Uses of the University (1963), also stressed the importance of knowledge, but he stressed *new* knowledge, born out of original research, not merely the dissemination of *received* knowledge as in Newman's university[7]. Kerr extended Newman's point about multiple fields of activity focusing upon another key point to today's institution in their engaging with actors, issues and interests beyond the university (what we now refer to as stakeholders) and their goals. He framed universities as 'multiversities' – like the universities we know now, which undertake a range of activities and engage *inter alia* industry and the communities around them[8].

In a regional context this foregrounds the fundamental importance of knowledge to external actors and the relevance of a university experience to a broad range of professions and careers. This is not just knowledge for its own sake. However, as Marginson argues, Kerr's account lacks two key elements, and these are especially relevant to this discussion of universities in regions; firstly, that revenue goals have come to drive the universities' priorities; secondly (he argued) is a lack of focus upon the individual learner[9]. Today, however, commercialisation dominates the discourse of a university and students are viewed as fee-paying customers; today it can be argued that the commercial imperative of students as consumers has forced a focus upon students as customers. Collini[10] insists that an experiment is being carried out on higher education institutions in England which are increasingly subject to market forces. As we shall see, market forces in the higher education sector are leading many universities to adopt a principally regional, as well as international, focus.

Today's university operates on a number of scales – local, national and international. This is consistent with notions of governance which suggest that the focus of public institutions today is no longer the nation state, but a multiplicity of levels of decision-making and authority. Shaped by the dynamics of globalisation and embedded in global flows of intellectual, financial, digital and human resources, Kerr's 'multiversities' have evolved into the 'global research university'[11]. It has been argued that, operating in the global knowledge economy, and encouraged by governments, there has been a shift in the idea of a university from sites "...of critical inquiry and autonomous learning..." to operating as international commercial organisations existing in competitive global markets[12]. In today's knowledge economy individuals and institutions require knowledge resources and there has been significant qualifications inflation. The consequential 'massification' of higher education has resulted in (growth statistics in here of students...) and this demand has created pressures on the university as new players have entered the sector. Today, higher education is not the sole preserve of the university as a range of new institutions in this sector, including higher education colleges and private sector organisations as well as other academic providers like further education colleges, move into higher education, offering degrees though without the depth or breadth of a 'traditional' university with its research basis. Moreover, the geography of presence does not conform with the geography of provision as providers sometimes use new modes and forms of delivery to a diversity and plurality of students within a competitive, crowded and contested arena with course delivery operating to global student communities.

Moreover, the new funding environment, based upon income from self-funded students and more commercial, industry-led research, is creating pressures on universities to shift their entire approach into a more 'customer-facing' and applied orientation. At the same time, the requirements of students for enhanced employability and the immediate career relevance of qualifications is also leading to a significant shift in the character of universities. Reflective detachment has been replaced by real world relevance as a key element of the marketing of courses and many universities, new and old alike, as they compete for customers in the new commercialised higher education environment.

In this new environment the orientation of many universities has changed, shifting the former focus upon research and teaching towards their region[13]. This refocus has increasingly anchored a university to its place. Regions regard universities as key enablers of regional performance through their role in the attraction of inward investment, and through industry in regions by providing supplies of skilled labour. Their operating as 'attractors, educators and retainers of students'[14] is promoted as a key part of the regional impact of a university.

In the globalised, knowledge-based economy the presence of a research university is seen as a key asset in the economic future of a region[15]. This perspective has come to shape the funding and strategies of many higher education institutions which aim to address a regional agenda. As a consequence of a decline in government funding for science research and increased competition for students, regionally driven funding for innovation and access universities to look for other sources of funds and find them in regional settings.

Consistent with this, the 'triple helix' (3H) model of innovation which describes interactions between universities, industry and government, foregrounds the role of science and technology in regional development and especially the role of a university and its technology transfer[16]. This echoes more traditional models of tripartite collaboration between the state, industry and educational institutions which have stronger roots in continental European countries, namely Germany and the Nordic states. Today, in regional development, universities are at the core of knowledge-based economies. From a regional perspective much of the power of the 3H model actually highlights the role of place, of the context of the network of interactions played out in the intersection of the helices within a region. The power of the interactive dynamic within the 3H model derives from proximity and from interactions between individuals within a region and the creative 'spark' engaging the helices through institutional, interpersonal interactions and communications. The essentials of the 3H process are described by Etzkowitz and Leydesdorff as being...

> ...driven by individuals and groups who make conscious decisions as well as the appearance of unintended consequences. A 3H in which each strand may relate to the other two can be expected to develop an emerging overlay of communication networks and organisations among the helices. . . . Regionally-based network of relations can... generate a reflexive sub-dynamic of intentions, strategies, and projects that adds surplus value...[17]

Essentially, the 3H process is one of constant dialogue between individuals from the three sectors leading to innovation and the emergence of mode three knowledge[18]. Of special relevance to this discussion is that the context within which these interactions occur is increasingly seen as fundamental to the process – especially for regional development and indeed from a university's standpoint may, in some cases even be a reason for a regional or sub-regional presence. Conceptual development of the 3H model is especially relevant to our discussion here as it foregrounds the importance of a regional setting.

Drawing upon Carayannis et al the quadruple helix model locates the 3H dynamic within the public sphere – media and culture-based public and civil society[19]. This focus upon the wider social and cultural context begins to connect the innovation process with its social and economic context. A further conceptual development, the fifth helix, stresses the wider, ecological context of interactions[20]. In the field of sustainable development the influence of the environment upon interactions, and the nature of human interactions with the natural environment, especially regarding the economy, has a strong influence upon the nature of interactions within the innovation process. This fifth element in the helix model is not so much about direct influence upon interactions between, but gives how an appreciation of values in the public sphere – the cultural context within which the axial relationships between universities, industry and government in regional (or sub-regional settings) can come to shape these interactions. These interactions, and the geographies of interactions and geometries of power relationships, which may even shape the institutional context as the innovators, and their institutions themselves come to change through their innovations[21]. These new institutional structures, which may span intellectual, commercial and geographical boundaries, will almost certainly include a university or universities within their network.

Essentially, the 5H model foregrounds the context of the interactions, and the relationship between actors within their wider social, cultural and environmental setting. In the context of the role of universities in regional development, the 5H model firmly locates interactions with the university sector as a key driver of regional development and innovation, but it makes an essential point about wider influences in the creation of knowledge. Essentially, through the interactions within the 3H, the codified mode one knowledge of the university becomes operationalised, engaging the tacit knowledge of the public sphere into problem-solving and application. It may be that the proximity of the actors, within a common culture, heritage and environment, highlights the potential influence of place upon the actual innovation process itself and foregrounds the regional setting. The influences upon those interactions in the wider democratisation of knowledge, from the 'mode one' knowledge of the university, through its application as mode three, which intertwines mode one and mode two knowledge as the codified knowledge of the academic sphere merges with the tacit knowledge of professional practice and lay insights, democratising the knowledge process and focusing it upon the local. The regional impact of a university may be broad indeed as it acquires and fixes codified global, 'mode one' knowledge in an amalgamation of the global codified knowledge piped into a region by the university through its academic network and local faculty and forging it into new structures of innovation.

The relationship between different modes of knowledge may be key to understanding the impact of a university in a region in knowledge development and innovation. The role of a university in innovation is central as the development of new knowledge in an increasingly complex environment requires both close and distant interactions[22] as local tacit knowledge derived from local and proximate interactions melds with codified knowledge from the academic sphere for which a university acts as a global 'pipeline'. But in addition to that role as a conduit, another key element within the helix dynamic is the local 'buzz' created by the interactions between participants within the region, between the helices, and here the university can have an important role. This dynamic may be being shaped by the characteristics of the region which bear upon the nature of interactions between the helices, and in some regions those interactions may be dominated by a certain sector or controlled by actors who set 'rules of the game' which privilege or deny access. The character of a region and its social and cultural elements and character which influence the wider innovation process and set an agenda which may also be influenced by the governance of a region. As we shall see later in the book, the geography of teaching and research provision may not coincide with administrative or cultural conceptions of regional geographies and may, in some cases, be a factor in rescaling the economic geography of a region.

It may be that the uniqueness of their regional setting and its economic and demographic profile, geography and heritage creates significant opportunities for universities operating in those contexts in respect of access to markets. But also a university, or university campus, strongly influenced by its regional setting, can also shape its content and character, which can give unique perspectives upon issues and agendas which would be unavailable without that view. But there are tensions, too, and there are also imperatives to work in new ways – all of which can dilute the very idea of the university in these settings as the university pursues a regional, commercial agenda.

There is, though, something about the breadth of a 'traditional' conception of a university consistent with Clark Kerr's own conception of a broad 'multiversity'[23]. Scale, both in terms of depth and breadth, gives a university a particular quality. Today, perhaps because of that potential breadth, the role of a university is becoming less clear as universities pursue multiple goals simultaneously. With competing regional demands and expectations, a risk of pursuing a regional agenda is a shift from the core business associated with scholarship and research, into commercially focused subjects with a regionally focused end use.

Today, universities are also involved in many spheres of activity and levels of education, from schools outreach to leading-edge science. Their impact extends into most corners of communities and may touch the lives of individuals who do not actually attend university; the entrepreneurial culture of institutions interacts with individuals, issues and interests. In this book we see how they give prestige to a city and enhance the reputation of a region. In respect of regional development they can make significant contributions to most aspects of regional life at individual and institutional levels. Universities can be part of a local 'buzz' and through their knowledge networks they fix intellectual capital and resources for innovation in regions.

Today, new modes of knowledge and models of knowledge development foreground the setting within which the innovation process is situated. Indeed, the role of universities as engines of growth and development come to play a key part in the development of new applied knowledge and innovation through a creative dialogue between the university and a region's unique synthesis of individual and institutional linkages they provide. In an era of homogenisation and with the emergence of global measures and models of success in the form of global league tables, the regional setting of universities and their associated relational assets may give these institutions a creative edge as well as access to regional markets.

NOTES

1. Davies, 1997, page 30; Bramwell and Wolfe, 2008, page 1175.
2. Markusen, 1996.
3. Benneworth and Jongbloed, 2010, page 567.

4. Chatterton and Goddard, 1999.
5. Shore, 2010, page 16.
6. Newman 1852, xxviii.
7. Marginson, 2008, page 1.
8. Marginson, 2008, page 5.
9. Marginson, page 6.
10. Collini, 2012.
11. Marginson, 2014, page 17.
12. Shore, 2010, page 15.
13. Goddard and Chatterton, 1999, cited in Gunasekara, 2004, page 229.
14. Gunasekara, 2004, page 330.
15. Bramwell, et al 2008, page 1175; Neave, 1979, cited in Davies, 1997, page 29.
16. Etzkowitz and Leydesdorff, 2000, page 109.
17. Etzkowitz and Leydesdorff 2000, pages 112–113.
18. Carayannis et al, 2012, page 4.
19. Carayannis 2012, page 13.
20. Carayannis et al, 2012, page 17.
21. Etzkowitz et al, 2000, page 114.
22. Bathelt et al, 2004, page 40.
23. Clark Kerr, 1963.

REFERENCES

Bathelt, H, Malmberg, A. and Maskell, P. (2004) Clusters and Knowledge: Local Buzz, Global Pipelines and the Process of Knowledge Creation. *Progress in Human Geography* Vol. 28, No. 1 Pages 31–56.

Benneworth, P. S. and Jongbloed, B. W. A. (2010) Who Matters to Universities? A Stakeholder Perspective on Humanities, Arts and Social Sciences Valorisation. *Higher Education* Vol. Pages 59 567–588.

Bramwell, A. and Wolfe, D. A. (2008) Universities and Regional Economic Development: The Entrepreneurial University of Waterloo. *Research Policy* No. 37 Pages 1175–1187.

Carayannis, E. and Campbell, D. F. J. (2012) Mode 3 Knowledge Production in Quadruple Helix Innovation Systems Springer *Briefs in Business* No. 7.

Carayannis, E. G., Barth, T. D. and Campbell, D. F. J. (2012) The Quintuple Helix Innovation Model: Global Warming as a Challenge and Driver for Innovation. *Journal of Innovation and Entrepreneurship* Vol. 1, No. 2.

Collini, S. (2012) What is the University For? London: Penguin.

Davies, J. L. (1997) The Regional University: Issues in the Development of an Organisational Framework. *Higher Education Management* Vol. 9 No. 3.

Etzkowitz, H. and Leydesdorff, L. (2000) The Dynamics of Innovation: from National Systems and "Mode 2" to a Triple Helix of University–Industry–Government Relations. *Research Policy* Vol. 29, Issue 2, Pages 109–123.

Goddard, J.B. and Chatterton, P. (1999) Regional Development Agencies and the Knowledge Economy: Harnessing the Potential of Universities. *Environment and Planning C. Government and Policy* Vol. 17 Pages 685–699. Cited in Gunasekara, 2004, Page 229.

Gunasekara, C. (2004) The Third Role of Australian Universities in Human Capital Formation. *Journal of Higher Education Policy and Management*, Vol. 26, No. 3 Pages 329–343.

Kerr, C. (2001) The Uses of the University. Fifth Edition. Cambridge: Harvard University Press. First published 1963.

Marginson, S. (2014) Teaching and Research in the Contemporary University. In Geoscience Research and Education: Teaching at Universities. Editor Vincent C. H. Tong, Volume 20 of the series Innovations in Science Education and Technology, Springer. Pages 11–18.

Marginson, S. (2008) Clark Kerr and the Uses of the University. Unpublished Paper presented at the CSHE Ideas and Issues in Higher Education seminar, 15 December 2008. Retrieved from http://www.cshe.unimelb.edu.au/research/res_seminars/issues_ideas/2008/docs/Clark-Kerr15Dec08.pdf.

Markusen, A. (1996) Sticky Places in Slippery Space: A Typology of Industrial Districts. *Economic Geography*, Vol. 72, No. 3 Pages 293–313.

Neave, G. (1979) Education and Regional Development: An Overview of a Growing Controversy, *European Journal of Education* Vol. 14 No. 3. Pages 207–231.

Newman, J. H. (1982) *The Idea of a University.* Notre Dame: University of Notre Dame Press. First published 1852.

Shore, C. (2010) Beyond the Multiversity: Neoliberalism and the Rise of the Schizophrenic University. *Social Anthropology* Vol. 18, No. 1 Pages 15–29.

A NEW ROLE FOR UNIVERSITIES IN POST-BREXIT BRITAIN?

Maddalaine Ansell

The Brexit vote revealed a deep ambivalence about many aspects of British society. It is hard to disentangle the many threads of unease but they include frustration that the benefits of globalisation are unequally distributed, concern that economic goals too often trump societal wellbeing and a rejection of a world order in which decisions are made by organisations that are remote from the people they serve.

This last point is not new. The devolution agenda in the United Kingdom has been driven by the recognition that people in the different nations of Britain and regions of England believe that power is too concentrated in London. Real change, however, has been very slow. John Prescott's attempt to create regional assemblies in 2004 faltered because he could not get his colleagues in government to let go of enough power. It took the Scottish referendum on independence in 2014 – and the subsequent concern that the devolved nations were getting a better deal than the English regions – to shake loose Whitehall's grip. Brexit has provided a new burning platform. Many cities now have a metro mayor and a growth deal.

This presents an opportunity to address the big questions about how we want to live, work and share wealth.

Universities are well placed to contribute – more than 150 are distributed throughout the UK from the Highlands and Islands of northern Scotland to Falmouth in the English south-west. Many see themselves as 'anchor institutions'. They do not move out of a region when times are tough, but they are not parochial. They recruit most of their staff and students from their region and work mainly with the businesses and communities around them. But they also have the scale to act nationally and internationally and the balance sheet to hold funding for projects involving many partners. Importantly, they have the longevity to look beyond the political priorities of the day and take long-term strategic action.

Last year, University Alliance looked at the role of universities in their cities and regions through four different lenses: health, skills, innovation and opportunity. These reports can be found at www. unialliance.ac.uk.

Universities are already recognised as significant contributors to the UK economy. Since Harold Wilson's 'white heat' speech at the 1963 Labour party conference, policymakers have recognised that Britain is a small island with limited natural resources but lots of people. It must create a place for itself in the world through building a knowledge economy. This must be driven by the creation and exploitation of knowledge and by skilled and innovative people. Universities are crucial to both.

This vision works when looked at through the lens of opportunity for individuals too. University can help people to find a desirable and fulfilling place in society. By becoming skilled, they have a higher value within the knowledge economy and can compete for jobs that might be interesting, well paid and socially valuable, or some combination of all three.

This telling of the story of the value of universities to the nation has been dominant for some years – but the Brexit vote suggests that it does not work for everyone. There are many people who see universities as part of the elite that benefits from globalisation, cut off from the concerns of those that do not. When Michael Gove said, "people in this country have had enough of experts", it was widely reported because it contained a kernel of truth. Many people do not believe that the nation's expertise is put at their service.

So universities need to create a new narrative in which their role in economic growth (important though this is) is balanced with improved social wellbeing.

The two will, of course, often be closely linked. General Electric Aviation has its global base for engine overhaul in south Wales supported by its partnership with the University of South Wales. The university agreed to integrate the industry standard aircraft maintenance qualification into its honours degree, enabling General Electric Aviation to recruit people with the qualifications it needs. This has created high-quality jobs in the region so that people can stay and bring up families with a good standard of living. There are many examples of universities being the key factor that keeps globally mobile business investment in the UK.

Universities also have the size and scale to work with small and medium-sized businesses, which may not have their own research and development or partnership teams. For example, Nottingham Trent University, the University of Nottingham and the University of Derby, as part of the D2N2 LEP Growth Hub, are working with more than 2,000 businesses in the Derby and Nottingham areas to boost their innovation. Among other things, they are creating technical hubs in food and drink, materials engineering, computing and data and design innovation. This is underpinned by European Structural and Investment Funds – the universities have the expertise to deal with complex bidding processes and the balance sheet to hold large sums of money for the benefit of multiple partners.

Work is, of course, a core part of social wellbeing. Many of us spend most of our waking lives at work and so we want it to be fulfilling and to align with our values. We want to make a difference. This is a significant challenge but there are cases where universities have used their international connections to explore new ideas about how we work which can inform this discussion. For example, Preston has suffered from the decline of its traditional cotton industries. Cotton jobs have gone and no alternative anchor industry has taken their place. The University of Central Lancashire, working with Preston City Council, has looked overseas to find out how other cities have dealt with the same challenge. They became particularly interested in worker cooperatives in Cleveland, Ohio in America's rust belt and in Mondragon in the Spanish Basque region. They are now thinking about how these models might work in the context of the English north-west.

The identity of a place is important. People want to be proud of where they live. They support their sports teams and boast about anything that makes them special. I used to have a friend from Colchester who would tell me every time I visited that their station platform was the longest in Britain (she was very disappointed to learn that this is disputed). Universities can play a key role in cementing and promoting this identity. The symbol of the city of Coventry, which was reborn from the ashes of the Blitz, is a phoenix. The university was inspired by the city's pride in its history to set up a Centre for Peace, Trust and Social Relations. This draws on expertise from across the social sciences to tackle challenges such as re-establishing peaceful societies following conflict, tackling piracy and exploring positive social relations in communities suffering from economic depression. In so doing, it gives the city's experience new meaning.

The Brexit referendum result made it impossible to pretend that Britain is working for everyone. The problem is complex and resolution is likely to take time. Universities have the potential to make a tremendous contribution.

TOWARDS THE VERY MODEL OF A MODERN UNIVERSITY

Mike Thomas

The University of Central Lancashire is nearly 200 years old and can trace its roots and heritage back to its establishment as the Institution for the Diffusion of Knowledge which was first proposed in the Preston Chronicle newspaper on 23 August 1828 by local activist Joseph Livesey. In Preston the population had grown to three times its size in 30 years thanks to the huge growth of the cotton industry. Its population was only 12,000 in 1801 but had risen to 33,000 by 1831[1] and the need for an apprenticeship institute was clear.

Preston had always had an important social role to play in the north-west. In the 18th century it was the centre where many of the county legal cases were heard, a meeting place for the upper classes with large estates and much of the commercial elite had started to settle in the town as industrialisation grew in speed and size. That mixture of the landed gentry with the manufacturing class ensured that Preston retained a dominant place in the social, religious and cultural life of the region. One aspect of the rapid industrialisation in England and Scotland was the growth of the Mechanics Institute which had been established in the areas of most dense industrialisation. Sheffield, Liverpool, Birmingham, Manchester, Leeds, Glasgow and Edinburgh all had Mechanics and Apprentice Libraries in place by the first third of the 19th century. These all attempted to

provide free education for children alongside those usually provided
for by religious organisations, plus education for those in work from
the age of 12 onwards. Funding came from subscriptions from local
middle-class, mainly, men. Livesey, a cheesemonger in Preston, had
been working with Sunday school projects and newspaper rooms
since around 1815 and eventually proposed the Institute for the Diffusion of Knowledge in 1828. Pope and Phillips[2] suggest that the
exclusion of the word 'mechanics' was an attempt by Livesey and
a local surgeon John Gilbertson, (who provided books and equip-
ment), to broaden support from local gentlemen and to bring different elements of society together. Livesey issued a circular in the
town and the first meeting, on 11 September 1828, was held above
Mr Templeton's school at 11 Cannon Street where a provisional
committee was formed and chaired by Gilbertson.

The inaugural meeting of the Preston Institute for the Diffusion
of Knowledge was held on 7 October 1828 at the Corn Exchange.
Twenty-four people were there (11 gentlemen and 13 operatives),
and they formed the first council of the institution. Shortly after-
wards on, 15 November, at its first open meeting, Thomas Addison
was elected its first president, Robert Ashcroft as secretary and
Livesey as the treasurer. Looking back in time it is interesting to see
the ambition and scale of thinking of that first group. The president
had suggested that the new London University that had recently
been formed might be something that could be done in Preston, and
later strong links were established. The initial annual subscription
costs to be a member of the institute was between 10s and 6d and
£1,1s a year (equivalent to 52p and £1 in modern currency) and
members were allowed extra tickets for admission to lectures. The
minimum subscription was 1s 7½d (approximately 8p) a quarter or
6s,6d (32p) a year. One has to remember that male cotton workers
in the factories earned under £1 a week, women much less and yet
despite this between 1828 and 1829 the institute had between 600
and 800 subscribers, was open most afternoons and evenings Mon-
day to Saturday and paid for a full-time librarian. By the end of the
1830s the institute had 3,000 volumes and by the turn of the 1870s

over 11,000 and was reputed to be one of the best provincial libraries in England. People in Preston liked to read and the chance of a
free library which also provided daily newspapers, taxed at the time
and therefore out of the reach of those on low salaries, made it an
extremely popular venue for the locals. In the 1870s when Preston
opened its first free public library the membership and attendance
of the institution's library virtually disappeared overnight as people
flocked to the free access for books and newspapers. However, that
first 40 years of subscription payments helped establish the institute and without the library and the reading facilities it is doubtful
whether the institute would have survived. Certainly attendance at
lectures and public events was generally much poorer and this may
be related to the fact that it was only those who paid the higher
subscriptions who could access tickets or that the price at the door
was too high. By the 1840s lectures were mainly offered free and
subjects included chemical sciences, electricity, human anatomy
and physiology, and what would now been seen as plant biology,
mechanics and astronomy. Teaching, however, was an extremely
small aspect of the institute's work. It was not possible to get regular
teachers at that time, but much more difficult was arranging time off
for apprentices time off from the cotton mills and their subcontrac-
tors. In addition, reading, writing and mathematics were mainly
provided by local church groups, many of which did not take kindly
to the teaching aspirations of the institute. By the early 1850s much
of the working classes and apprentices had actually developed their
own teaching and reading groups and were instructing each other on
how to read and write and also using the gatherings for the awareness of social issues and collective rights. The institute was therefore seen by many from the working classes of Preston as one that
belonged to professional gentlemen and local commercial owners.
This lack of working-class participation, despite being the obvious
aims of many of the mechanics institutes, was not confined to Preston but was beginning to be widespread across England.

By the 1850s the Institute had moved into its Avenham Building
in Preston but was beginning to face problems in membership and

the delivery of education to the working classes. This can be seen by the fact that by the 1850s the population of Preston had grown to 80,000 but the membership of the institute remained as it had for the past 30 years, at approximately 600. In the late 1850s the committee took the radical decision to make classes free and this appeared to have some success. A teacher was brought in on a fixed salary of £20 a year in the early 1860s and separate classes for girls and young women were established in 1865. For the younger age group the institute provided reading, writing, dictation, arithmetic, grammar and composition, English and history, but attendance was still low. Despite the fact that by now a law had been passed (the 1847 Factory Act) to restrict the working day to 10 hours it was still difficult for workers to attend classes during the day and the institution decided to move to both day and evening classes. The institute was once again facing some difficulties in the area of teaching by the 1870s. No male teacher was available for the whole of 1872 and from 1874 there were no female classes available. One way of addressing this was for wider links and in the latter half of the 19th century the Institute began links with the School of Design in Manchester which then became the Preston School of Art. In the 1870s the institute also had links with the science school and, despite the mass recession in the cotton industry at the time, (due to the American Wars and the blockade in the Americas to prevent cotton reaching England), both the arts school and the science school began to achieve some success, though as the century began to draw to a close both were always under threat of closure. The art and the science schools' impact on the town should not be underestimated. It was seen by many as rivalling those in large cities such as Manchester and London and many national prizes were won through those years. Over 800 young people were submitted for science and art department examination by the mid 1870s and many of the teaching classes were once again offered in the evenings only. In the final year of its teaching, 1880 and 1881, 328 students were studying at the institute.

The need for income meant that the institute was constantly appealing to the town's Harris Trustees for money. It was expensive, sometimes for up to £25,000. In 1881 the Harris Institute allocated £40,000 for the promotion of arts, literature and the advancement of technical education in the town and had its ambition to rival Manchester's Owens College and Sheffield's Firth College, both of which went on to become the University of Manchester and Sheffield respectively. This new injection of funding plus the established work of the institute alongside the arts and science Schools gave some impetus. 520 students were enrolled into the first year and a staff of 12 was established. One evening course enrolled 101 students in science studying magnetism and electricity and in mathematics more than 50 students were enrolled. By 1883/1884 1300 students were in the Harris Institute in Preston. The Avenham Building was given £5,000 to upgrade its accommodation, particularly to ensure that there were larger classrooms. As the century came to a close over 2,000 students were enrolled and more students were passing technical subjects at honours level than did students from similar institutions in London, Birmingham, Glasgow or Edinburgh. In 1889 only the Birkbeck Institute, London and the Liverpool Institute had more students passing its exams in the whole of England and it was not just elementary arts or science subjects that were now being taught; brickwork, masonry and plumbing came in as the building trades advanced. Agriculture was also now being provided and the first classes in nursing were organised with the St John Ambulance Association with the institute having its own Ambulance Corps. As the century turned more than 4,000 individual students enrolled at the institute and more than 60 staff were on its books, many employed full time.

Lancashire had established its own County Council by this point and in 1893 the chairman of the new Lancashire County Council observed that Harris' range of growth and the generalisation of its curriculum suggested that it was a polytechnic and the college was claiming that it should be compared to Owens College Manchester and University College Liverpool. The institute had its own professor of chemistry, it had its own School of Domestic Science, it had an agricultural department funded by Lancashire County Council in

1891 and classes in law taught by local barristers, although a law school in its own right was not established until the 1970s. The institute was now spreading across the town; the new Jubilee Technical School was established in Corporation Street (what is today known as the Harris Building in the university). The reorganisation of the School of Domestic Science meant that there was accommodation in Glovers Court. Alterations in the Avenham Building included a fully equipped physics laboratory and the Engineering School was developing with bequests from local large firms. The Harris Institute was affiliated to the Victoria University in Manchester which had within its federation the Owens College, the University College Liverpool and the Yorkshire College at Leeds. This allowed students to prepare for the London University Matriculation Exams and for final BA and BSc examinations as well as undertaking the Victoria University preliminary access programmes.

As the First World War came into sight both Manchester and Liverpool Universities were now separate universities but still held seats on the Harris Institute Council and students were gaining full degrees within the college. By 1914 the Harris Institute was firmly established in the town with a staff of 80 (including 24 women), 30 employed fulltime. It had eight heads of departments, 22 assistant teachers, over 3,000 students and was once again offering day courses. Understandably, the First World War led to a decline in its student and staff bodies as many were called away to service, but after 1918 the institute continued to develop, particularly in areas of engineering with the recently established Leyland Motors a few miles away, the Elementary Science Provision, nurses for the Preston Royal Infirmary and engineering for the agricultural industry.

Changes in legislation in the late 1920s meant that much more control of education was taken by the county councils and one benefit for the Harris Institute was the extension of the Jubilee Technical School in Corporation Street which was funded by the county council. Despite the severe recession in the late 1920s and early 1930s the county council continued to contribute to the new extensions for art and natural science laboratories and chemistry was moved from the Avenham Building to the Corporation Street site. New courses such as the ONC and the HNC in building, chemistry and economics were introduced. A new site in Hutton was provided in the 1930s and a three-year radio servicing course was introduced due to the local expansion of wireless manufacturers. Pharmacy was also now being introduced and degrees were still being offered through London University, particularly in engineering. The new apprentices at the Royal Ordinance Factory, Euxton and at Siemans Lampworks now began to attend for day and evening courses while a School for Managers was established for those still involved in the cotton trade.

After the Second World War, there was an anticipation that the college, particularly with the development of the Higher Level Technical awards would be developed into a university (University of the Fylde based in Preston) and this was seriously pursued by Preston City Council and the Harris Institute throughout the late 1940s. In the end it was decided that Preston would have a central college retaining the name Harris in the institute's title. The Harris College of Further Education was finally established on 4 April 1956. There was still a view regionally that the Harris College would gain university status but in the early 1960s the county council decided to follow a twin-track policy on higher education and a bid to establish a university in the county which would be complemented by the establishment of the Harris College as the first rank technical college. In 1966 the government decided to publish its plans for polytechnics and other colleges and decided that there would be just two institutes in the north-west. The Harris College leaders worked feverishly with the North West Regional Advisory Council and other bodies to push the Harris Council to be one of the foremost regional colleges and put forward a bid to gain polytechnic status. The North West Regional Advisory Council identified Preston's Harris Institute, the Bolton Institute of Technology and Stockport College as areas of particularly good provision and a regional request was submitted to the government for a further two polytechnics to be considered in the north-west, though this did not include the Harris Institute. There was also a plan for a joint Blackburn polytechnic where Blackburn

College of Technology and Design would merge with the Harris Institute. After all this intense dialogue and debate the final list by the government came out in April 1967. The government accepted that a further polytechnic institute could be provided in Lancashire as well as Staffordshire, but not the location and it was not until 1969 that it was finally agreed by the Department of Education and Science that the planning for a polytechnic in Preston should commence, particularly as Preston had new town designation. In 1973 the title Preston Polytechnic was eventually established.

From its establishment on 31 May 1973, the polytechnic continued to work closely with the regional county council and began to run campuses across Poulton-le-Fylde and Leyland and continued to have good arrangements with colleges in Blackburn and Blackpool. It also had libraries at Chorley and had a campus at Poulton, including the Woodland Annexe Library that was handed over to Edgehill College in 1981. Computer sciences joined the polytechnic provision in 1974 and health continued to develop. Services for students rapidly expanded with a students' union, careers advisory service and technical support. Art and design expanded, as did business and management, humanities and social studies alongside science and technology. The organisation was growing rapidly and on 7 November 1981 the Academic Development Committee of Preston Polytechnic first proposed a change of name. The polytechnic was no longer just based in Preston although clearly that was where the heart of its work mainly lay but it also delivered across the region and so in March 1983 the council gave its support to change its name. In September 1983 the secretary of state gave permission for the new name of Lancashire Polytechnic. By now the county-wide polytechnic had faculties of cultural, legal and social studies; of design and technology and health plus it had the Lancashire Business School and the Faculty of Science and had increased its overall student numbers to over 11,000. In 1991 the government higher education white paper (a new framework) finally came to the conclusion that there should be an end to the differentiation between those institutions called polytechnics and those funded separately and called universities. The National Council for National Academic Awards was abolished and the allocation of degree-awarding powers allowed polytechnics to be able to use the word 'university' in their title and this was enshrined in the 1992 Further and Higher Education Act. On 16 June 1992 the Privy Council approved the use of the title University of Central Lancashire which was allowed to award its own degrees, including research degrees. It was important for the binary difference between polytechnics and universities to be finally resolved. There was confusion among the business community, the commercial sector, prospective students and within education generally about the differentiation of missions and values. Many polytechnics shared similar values and had similar histories to well-established universities. For example, the University of Central Lancashire had its roots way back in the Harris Institute and before that the Institute for the Diffusion of Knowledge. But it shared its students and its awards with those colleges that went on, through separate journeys, to become the Universities of Liverpool, Manchester and Sheffield. Over the last 30 years as the university sector in the United Kingdom has settled down (over 132 institutions are now members of Universities UK), other education providers have come into the delivery of higher education provision. This is particularly prevalent in the last 15 years and does create some confusion for those outside the university or tertiary education sector.

WHAT IS A UNIVERSITY?

There are three sub-themes in relation to the question of 'what is a university' in modern UK society; why all economies create them; what defines a university; and how a university education improves public reasoning (capacity to make moral and technical judgements).

Universities UK (2015) states that universities have a hugely important economic role. They remain competitive in a global market and support greater business innovation and export-led-knowledge intensive growth. It also sees universities active in skills as the workforce changes in order to help the UK economy to increase its productivity overall. More and more universities are collaborating with employers to develop diverse and innovative pathways to higher level skills. Of 161 higher education institutes surveyed in the UK by the higher education business and community interaction survey, 108 offer continuous work-based learning and 150 universities offer bespoke courses for business on campus or on business premises. Universities support social mobility – between 2004 and 2013 the higher education participation rate of young people in the most disadvantaged areas of England actually increased by 43 per cent. Universities UK describes universities as 'anchor institutions' and ideal institutions to take the lead on significant social and economic issues at a local level by helping to shape local economic strategies, for example by supporting the local enterprise partnership, in the development of the European Structural Investment Fund Strategy, by linking research and teaching priorities to local economic and social needs and promoting public engagement, community well-being and active citizenship skills. Universities also play a role as global ambassadors and particularly as investment links both in and out of the local areas. In 2011–12 universities across the UK generated a total of £73 billion in output and directly contributed over £36.4 billion to the UK GDP and off-campus expenditure of international students and visitors contributed a further £3.5 billion. In total universities contribute nearly £40 billion to the UK GDP, equivalent to 2.8 per cent of GDP in 2011. This is more than the total numbers of health, construction and public administration. Higher education in the UK exports over £10.7 billion of export earnings. For every £1 million of university output a further £1.5 million of output is generated elsewhere in the economy. In GVA terms this means for every £1 million of university GVA, a further £3 million is generated in other UK universities. Nearly 760,000 full-time jobs are found in and generated by the higher education sector combined in 2011 and 2012. For every 100 jobs created within a university 117 other jobs are created elsewhere in the economy. None-university employment supported by universities equate to about 63,000 full-time jobs in

2011–12. In terms of employer satisfaction, the source used in the UUK report by CBI Pearson reveals that employer satisfaction with graduate skills compared with school leavers' skills show nearly 100 per cent of employers satisfied with IT, over 90 per cent with team-working and self-management resilience and over 80 per cent with basic literature, use of English and numeracy skills.

More locally the Lancashire Strategic Economic Plan[3] key programmes and policies are summarised as seeking £11 million in competitive Growth Deal Funding to improve the capability and capacity of Lancashire's competitive strength, particularly in aerospace, automotive and energy and building up the capital centre of the Lancashire Enterprise Zone in Samlesbury. The plan also supports the development of a major research and innovation programme to enable Lancaster University and the University of Central Lancashire to expand and develop national centres of excellence linked to the delivery of local economic priorities. In skills development there is a Competitive Growth Deal funding to do a Skills for Growth programme, particularly in the apprenticeship hub and more SME engagement plus funding from competitive Growth Deal funding to form an enhanced business growth hub, particularly to support SMEs. There is strategic identification of £30 million in Competitive Growth Deal funding for the economic regeneration of Lancashire which includes a strategic transport programme of £195.7 million funding to be released particularly about economic and housing growth in Preston, east Lancashire and west Lancashire plus £26.6 million to renew the area of Blackpool.

This is not surprising as Lancashire is one of the largest local economies in the north of England, valued at over £23 billion, home to over 40,000 businesses employing in excess of 600,000 people from a population of 1.4 million. The region continues to see aerospace as one of its key industries that requires support alongside the automotive industry and the energy industry. New developing sectors include health, aerospace, food manufacturing, visitor economy, business and financial services. The readily identified economic hotspots for growth are the cities of Preston and Lancaster, but overall the economy lags behind other regions with the economy only growing by 4.4 per cent, compared to 6.5 per cent nationally. Its economic performance tends to be up to 20 per cent below the national average in terms of GBA per resident. However, it has three universities in its area, with Lancaster ranked in the top 10 UK universities for research and teaching, UCLan the fifth university in the country in terms of its undergraduate intake and the first modern university to be ranked in the QS world rankings. Edge Hill University won the prestigious University of the Year in 2015. It also has a number of outstanding further education provision in the district.

It's no wonder that commercial organisations are interested in the sector. However, it must be clear when considering these new market players that there is a difference between '**universities**' which is a legitimate and legally enshrined title awarded by, at present, the Privy Council and '**higher education**' providers. Higher education providers are those organisations that provide undergraduate or postgraduate programmes of some descriptions, but the awards themselves are provided by a **university** that already has teaching degree-awarding powers. When an institution or organisation wishes to hold the university title it must go through a process of auditing by the Quality Assurance Agency and meet conditions outlined under the 1992 Higher Education Act through which they can first of all apply for the title Teaching Degree Awarding Powers (TDAPs). Separately they apply to the Privy Council for the title university. Usually they go hand in hand, as the QAA currently reports to the Privy Council Sub-Committee on the outcome of their TDAPs reviews. Many further education colleges are now getting TDAPs (or Foundation Degree Awarding Powers) approval but are not going forward for university title. Equally, many commercial sector organisations have been allowed to have TDAPs but have not been put forward for university title.

Previous regulations stipulated a minimum of 4,000 higher education students enrolled to be considered for TDAPs but this number was dropped to 1,000 during the coalition government's period of office. BIS currently want to introduce a system where the numbers fall below than 1,000 so that any organisation with a few students studying at degree level can go forward for teaching degree awarding powers. BIS are also suggesting an alternative route to the QAA review where they go directly through BIS and be done much quicker, the proposal is within 18 months whereas the current TDAPs process can take between five and 12 years. Some organisations may go to the Privy Council and ask for the title 'university' or 'university college' or 'university institute' or 'university institutes of higher learning'. These options may confuse the sector but today the main differentiation between a university and a higher education provider can be summarised as follows: although an organisation may have teaching degree-awarding powers known as TDAPs most then go on to request Research Degree Awarding Powers (RDAPs). Those current organisations that call themselves 'universities', but only have TDAP authority cannot run postdoctoral research programmes or award PhDs unless they are validated and approved and awarded by a university that has RDAPs. For example, Glyndwr University, which was previously the North East Wales Institute of Higher Education, was awarded teaching degree-awarding powers and went to the Privy Council and altered its name from the North East Wales Institute of Higher Education to Glyndwr University. However, to date it is not approved to award its own research degrees and research degree-awarding power is held by the University of Chester.

Many commercial organisations do not see the benefit of having research-active staff within their organisation particularly if their activities are in low resource-intensive areas such as humanities, business or law. Engineering, science, technology, medicine, health care etc. need a vast amount of investment, are research-intensive and usually integral to research degree-awarding powers. Therefore, one of the major differences between a university and a higher education provider is the issue of being research-active on an equal basis with delivering teaching provision.

Many of the higher education providers, including further education colleges but mainly those in the commercial sector, do not have a charitable arm although some may have a not-for-profit status where revenue is put in to their own organisation. Nevertheless, a university is seen as an anchor institution in its community where it provides economic support, employment, are research and teaching active and have an important charitable function. Those entering the higher education market do not see themselves as representatives or integral to the community; many courses will be offered online, many are based in London, many will have head offices and buildings that are leased, rented and moved around, often globally. There is a significant difference between a university in terms of its locality and a higher education provider which moves its provision from one geographical location to another for commercial reasons. Universities are not like the commercial sector and neither are they like the public sector although some elements of public sector regulations do appear in the university sector because the university sector deals with a large amount of public money. Many universities which have charitable status have to demonstrate beneficiaries from any income raised through their activities. That money must be shown to provide good use for beneficiaries and not earned for shareholders, increasing dividends or for-profit in the traditional commercial sense.

Newman looked at these issues as Preston's Institute for the Diffusion of Knowledge was reaching its 30th anniversary. In 1856 he proposed that a university should be engaged in public debate and involvement, community responsiveness, develop moral reasoning and study and instil personal confidence. Over a hundred years later (as Preston's college was engaged in university and polytechnic debates) the Robbins Committee on Higher Education[4] suggested that universities should provide instruction in skills, promote general powers of the mind and advancement of learning. They should also be leaders in the transmission of a common culture and common standards of citizenship. The views of both the Newman and Robbins Committee views remain strong and appear to have a global application. For example in 2004 the US Futures Project[5] suggested that a university should hold responsibility for student learning, encourage social mobility through attainment, support elementary and secondary education and conduct research. A university should also serve as society's critic and build civic engagement.

Universities retain huge importance in the social and intellectual development of its students. Universities are expected to defend freedom of speech (by law) which provides a base to improve critical faculties, understand the basis for evidence (validity, reliability, rationality, and generalisation) and tolerance and understanding of opposing views. Students are also supported to understand values and worth through cultural engagement and the humanities[6] to develop creativity and innovation skills[7], be self-critical and learn how to apply morals, responsibility, technical skills, entrepreneurial faculty[8] and address 'difficult' questions in a safe environment[9]. This means improvement of an individual's communication skills (verbal, non-verbal, technical, artistic) and generating ideas and discoveries (to build a better world)[10]. In essence to learn to face the 'Great Challenges' with common sense, attention to detail, teamwork and compassion[11].

UCLAN'S MISSION AND NEW MODEL

Like many universities, UCLan's mission is clear and states 'we create positive change in our students, staff, business partners and wider communities, enabling them to develop their full potential by providing excellent higher education, innovation and research.' The mission reflects our values and the historical view of a university and advocates the principles espoused by Newman[12] and the Robbins Committee[13] through the pursuit of excellence in all that we do, equality of opportunity for all, supporting the rights and freedoms of our diverse community, the advancement and protection of knowledge, freedom of speech and inquiry and supporting the health, safety and wellbeing of all. From its roots nearly 200 years ago, the university sees itself as an anchor institute where, within its strategic aims, the university will create an 'inspirational student experience, enabling people irrespective of their backgrounds to fulfil their potential, develop as global citizens and meet their life and career goals'. UCLan is innovative and entrepreneurial in its approach to research and knowledge exchange in order to maximise our positive social, environmental and economic impact, locally, nationally and globally.

The university is an interesting reflection of its regional base with over 37,000 students, 51 per cent of its students from lower socio-economic groups, 98 per cent from state schools and many students are the first generations to enter university. Yet it has provided studies in fashion and also journalism for nearly 50 years, nursing and healthcare for over 100 years and its background in the town of Preston with its history of the temperance movement, its Christian socialism and its growth from town to city can be seen in the way that the university has developed provision to meet relevant local and regional needs, its large engineering faculty being one such area. It has also developed its own medical school and has its own dental and pharmacy schools all of which contribute to the health and wellbeing of the local community. UCLan graduates add on average £24 million to the north-west economy every year through increased skills and productivity while the university itself contributes over £200 million to the north-west economy and is considered one of the largest employers in the city (it supports over 4,300 full-time non-university jobs locally and is the ninth largest undergraduate population of all UK universities). It has a major campus development in Burnley, east Lancashire, a smaller centre in Westlakes, a hub for humanitarian work through its campus in Cyprus and has been in China for over 30 years. Still, the university must constantly adapt and respond to the local economy. The public policy voice is a persistent reminder that the university must engage in areas such as employment, employability, high tech development and social mobility. It must continue to have a voice in the community, act as a hub for local and regional development and engage in community leadership as well as social enterprise. It must also meet the business voice with knowledge-based work, provide a high level, skilled labour force, entrepreneurial skills and to promote SME developments. The university has one of the most successful student start-ups in the UK with over 1,000 companies formed by the student body in the last three years, 75 per cent of which are still in business. It must be ready for big changes in technology, the large global approach to open access to its research data and the flip learning approach much preferred by students. And the pressure does not stop there: the university must meet the competition voice, the private and publicly funded organisations that wish to work with the university, its global curriculum, its competition with other institutes, particularly those not from the university sector, and the growing marketisation of education at tertiary level in the UK. Finally and most importantly the students must be given experiences in curriculum that allows them to have successful careers and employment, to give them the skills in teamwork, communications, innovation, to experience the work place and also to provide an environment where they learn about life values, culture and their part in their community.

UCLan has adapted to this new world and global communication by beginning first steps towards developing a new model. This new model takes the best of European university engagement such as those found in north-west Europe and Germany as well as the traditions of universities as anchor institutions in the UK. The term 'anchor institutions' has gained wider credence over the last decade in the UK and is an attempt by many to identify the university as an important player in the local economic and social life of its geographical situation. There are several theoretical models put forward from the simple 3H model which envisages a relationship between a university, the local business community and the local authorities, to additions to the 3H which involve an examination of the relationship of the university with its local authorities, its business communities, governments, policymakers, its global network and its environment.

THE UNIVERSITY AS AN ANCHOR INSTITUTION

The concept of the university as an anchor institution accepts some underlying activities and engagements which include being focused on the social and economic life of its geographical location, the university's physical and historical links and the commitment to its geographical future success[14]. There is also the view that the university engages fully in city and regional collaborations with engagement with policies, local government, LEPs, employers, FECs, fundholders and so on. To support the economy its research should be translational,[15] its procurement processes local, its skills specialisms (higher apprenticeships) focused on regional sectors and its engagement (values) involve cultural engagement and events[16].

There are different permutations to these underlying themes but at heart the anchor institution is seen as symbolic of the financial and civic contribution the university can provide to its local community. It is now well established that universities provide funding and revenue to the local economy, such as UCLan's contribution of over £200 million a year to the local community as well as creating jobs, either in the university itself or through its many sub-contracting and procurement routes. The Centre for Local Economic Strategies (2016) states that a good local economy provides a strong network between and across the public, commercial and social sectors. CLES looked at an anchor institution locally in Preston which obviously has great interest for UCLan. It says, in regards to Preston, that the key to a good local economy is protecting and developing the capital and general activity related to the anchor institution and that these activities are retained within the local economy as much as possible. It is interesting that in a more philosophical sense it talks about anchor institutions as institutions and organisations that both recruit from and serve the local economy which fits in with the values and philosophies of UCLan. One of the most important areas related to the social development of the local community is local procurement and ensuring that employment is created and that money is spent locally to support the community.

The university sector in general within the UK can be seen to play an important role in that simple model of contribution to the economy. But there are differences in standards and performance between universities that participate more fully in the leadership of their local civic bodies and engagement with businesses. For example, part of that engagement with the local community is the activities that universities have with further education college providers. UCLan is envisaging a new model where the university can work in a federated system with colleges who wish to join with the strategic mission and intent of the university (which includes its values and mission). For example, three or four colleges in the same geographical vicinity may work with a university and local employers, but one college can expend its energies concentrating on one specific industrial skillset (for instance, mechanical engineering), while another college concentrates its activities in another industrial sector, for instance construction or media. By sharing strategic vision there is a better and more efficient use of resources with potential for backup and specialist staff to be shared to support all institutions. The university is also examining with great interest the potential for students studying for degrees to pick up vocational programmes and awards from its further education partners. Rather than an employer taking a graduate who then has to go on to do an apprenticeship programme or employing somebody who has done a vocational programme to do a part-time degree it is envisaged that it is possible to provide both qualifications at point of exit. This is not too dissimilar to the government's vision for higher apprenticeships and these areas are being actively explored.

The new model would be the 'anchor university' deeply embedded in its local community, actively participating in its economic and civic life and providing leadership in those areas but also developing new models of learning for students that would engage both horizontal and vertical awards at exit in strategic partnership with further education colleges and employers. There are opportunities for the curriculum to be more flexible with the curriculum delivering more science subjects for those studying the arts and humanities or more business subjects for those studying science and technology and so on so that a more rounded student understands different perceptions, methodologies and approaches.

The new model stresses the need for partnership and collaboration at a local level. One looks at the UK, particularly in England, where it is very difficult to identify a regional university. For example, there are 42 higher education providers in London alone and it is hard to envisage any one of those having a regional influence outside of the city where many other universities are active. But universities such as the University of Hertfordshire have shown how they can support the regional economy. The University of Chester is the only university in the county of Cheshire (not including centres and off-site campus from other institutions) and has demonstrated its worth in supporting that community. It is now supporting the county of Shropshire with its university ambitions using the anchor model. The UCLan shares the county with the universities of Lancaster and Edge Hill and also works closely with the universities in the cities of Liverpool and Manchester. A regional university is probably best termed as that which can be defined as a collaboration between universities in a distinct geographical area which together provide opportunities and growth in that geographical locality.

THE FUTURE

It is clear that universities do differ from higher education providers although policymakers, social planners and successive government administrations are working hard to confuse that picture and integrate universities into an overall concept of higher education. However, some facts demonstrate the differences and also the increasing role of higher education in the delivery of vocational and educational provision in the UK but not necessarily research or playing a part as an anchor institution.

In 2013–14, 330 organisations provided access to higher education courses; 83 per cent were further education colleges; 44,685 students were studying for an access to higher education diploma of which only 420 were actually studying for this diploma in a university. For the university sector in England and Wales the vast majority of the student body consists of those aged 20–24 years (34 per cent), 25–29 years (20 per cent) with only 1 per cent over the age of 50, only 3 per cent over the age of 45 and only 13 per cent under the age of 19. 74 per cent of students are female, 26 per cent are male and 70 per cent complete their course. Of the 35,295 successful diploma-to-higher-education access students who went through UCAS to apply for universities, 70 per cent were accepted. Unsurprisingly the statistics stubbornly show that lower socio-economic backgrounds have the highest participation of access programmes to higher education while A-level students are still more likely in higher participation neighbourhoods. Those access-to-higher education diploma students were in order of declining numbers in areas such as subjects allied to medicine, social studies, biology, education, social science, business and law and it is striking that these figures show that there are fewer students going on to study science. There is a difference, however, between part time and full time. In terms of popularity, subjects allied to medicine, social studies and biological science are popular among full-time students. The data indicates a success story for widening participation universities with 30 per cent of students who complete their access to higher education diploma going on to have a lower second, but over 45 per cent going on to get an upper second class and just under 17 per cent of those student achieved a first class honours degree at exit. The trend for access to higher education via the diploma route continues to rise year on year as does the number of accepted applicants while the number of mature students continues to decline and is a concern for universities. Future medium-term provision growth appears to be in STEM subjects which may impact on access-route student numbers and will require significant university investment therefore providing potential space for less resource-intensive subjects to be offered by new market players to access-route students. In time the tide will turn towards arts and humanities and some universities may struggle to reclaim provision lost to new providers.

In the Education Risk Profile carried out by PWC[17] in terms of impact and likelihood and then declining the areas of sector concern are as follows: changes in government and/or policy remains very high, as does postgraduate and undergraduate recruitment home and overseas. Investment in IT, outcome of regulatory inspections, financial sustainability, student experience, income reductions, research income, pension deficit, reputation, estates and capital programmes investment have less impact and less likelihood but are still within the risk profile alongside partnership and collaboration, staff recruitment, regulatory compliance and staff engagement.

In a separate report PWC[18] identified the following as issues facing the university sector; the marketisation and student demand, particularly the removal of the student control and student fees and moving the trend towards students as 'consumers'. To further complicate the picture it also identified the financial sustainability and operating efficiency of universities, requirement for investment in IT, particularly around digital and cybersecurity, internationalisation strategies, UKVI compliance, business resilience and business expansion, data quality and accounting changes such as FRS102 and the new SORP Statements which all provide further risk to the current university sector. Such a list provides a map of the university landscape at least for the next five years and signals the present government's intent to categorise universities and higher education providers in the same instrumentalist education 'market'.

The higher education green paper currently being considered also demonstrates the conflation of universities and higher education providers. The paper can be structured into four broad areas: teaching excellence, quality and social mobility (including the Teaching Excellence Framework – TEF – scoring matrix), market entry and opening the sector up to new providers. There are also suggestions for changes in the sector infrastructure, including the creation of the Office for Students, and simplifying the research funding system. The likelihood is that the green paper will become a white paper.

The barrage of policy drivers continues to increase. A sector briefing paper, Media FHE Briefing Report 27[19], highlights that BIS needs to make an overall saving of £2.4 billion, a 17 per cent cut, up to 2019 and 2010. Most of the savings will come from a switch from maintenance grants to loans and the university teaching grant will be reduced by £120 million in cash terms. Student opportunity funds will be reviewed with the view that it will probably be cut. While maintenance loans for part-time students will be introduced from 2018–19, nursing student maintenance grants will be replaced by student loans but the age for new loans to postgraduates from 2016–17 will be raised to 60 years of age. All STEM subjects will have tuition loans extended to those students wishing to do a second degree from 2017–18. Science funding will be protected, but an apprenticeship levy will be introduced in 2017 at a rate of 0.5 per cent of an employer's pay bill. New enterprise zones have been created, including in smaller towns which will encourage university involvement in the local economy. Universities UK[20] has stressed that too much policy interference will have a negative impact on economic health. For example, in discussing regional growth, the benefits of place-based approaches to growth and specialisms in local areas which are able to identify and select priority areas (particularly in knowledge-based investment), and the abilities for universities to bring European structural investment fund strategies into the local economy, will all be affected with current proposals. The role that universities play in driving innovation, particularly around regional growth and project grant funding, underpinning infrastructure such as the HEIF grant and the investment in new and emerging growth quickly require a degree of freedom and less constraint from policy drivers in such high numbers.

Universities will survive and continue to be engaged in their locality, with or without government interference. For instance, Hardy[21] looked at the issues around business involvement and the LEPs, the LEP networks, LEPs and local government, LEPs and planning and LEPs and universities. Hardy sees the central role of the universities as being active in regions, particularly in terms of their contributions to the knowledge base and the regional innovation system. This could be in all areas, researchers, suppliers, manufacturers, service providers, entrepreneurs, end users, public research, industry and scientific development. All are involved in areas such as human capital, ideas, collaboration, market opportunities, new technological innovations and catalysts for driving transformation and the economy.

Universities are expected and are keenly enthusiastic to play a key role in defining regional strategy and embed the universities' own departments within the local economy and not just in the economic or commercial world. Universities also look at major societal challenges and play a role in contributing towards the low-carbon economy, working to deal with the aging population and translate innovative products into the public and private sector. The universities will continue to play a major role in supporting governments and national priorities and, as Hardy[22] points out, universities are globally engaged and can often bridge a gap between national and local approaches through economic development. Universities as anchor institutions in local economies are described by Hardy as 'major employers across a wide range of occupation, purchases of local goods and services and contributors to cultural life and the built environment of towns and cities. Local investment in the infrastructure of the university in support of its core business of research and teaching can therefore have a significant passive regional multiplier effect, even if the university is not actively supporting regional development'. There are four areas where the universities will continue to make active contributions: business innovation, human capital development, community development and the contribution to local capacity through engagement. When these four areas are integrated the authors argue that a university can be seen to occupying a proactive role in the regional development process. These are critical assets, particularly where the private sector is weak or small or there are low levels of research and development. The resources of the university therefore can have a disproportionate positive effect on the local economic growth and what is required are a range of mechanisms to ensure that that engagement can take place. It is clear that universities have a prominent future role in both finding and achieving European-funded programmes. Universities should therefore be seen as absolutely important anchor institutions in their geographical areas.

And it is not just the universities' abilities to help with cultural and community infrastructure locally and regionally but also the universities' abilities to support and be deeply involved and lead skills acquisitions for economic regeneration. For example, the BIS Research Paper 171 looked at Technical Apprenticeship Research and the need for and capacity to deliver STEM-related apprenticeship provision in England. The first signal indicating a basis for the apprenticeship and apprenticeship levy can be found in this paper with its data showing the lack of technical-related apprenticeships in the UK and the need for those to be driven by employers. Successive governments seem preoccupied with attempting to rectify any deficiencies that are seen in the FE sector which is often based on unfounded and hearsay experiences rather than hard evidence. The universities are pulled into this debate because the FE sector has a long history of having very good industrial and commercial links. Unfortunately, successive administrations' attempts to reach clarity merely resulted in confusion and interference very often in areas that seem to be working well and are recognised as such by employers. For example, Kelly[23] looks at the confusion between post level 3 qualifications which include HNCs, HNDs, foundation degrees, A-levels, baccalaureates, diplomas, foundation degrees. The paper attempts to declutter the sector and makes a call for the need for universities to engage in this area. The FE sector is currently going through much more profound changes that the university sector but clearly impacts on universities, particularly when attempting to address government objectives such as recruitment from low participation neighbourhoods. However, the future is not bleak: government structures, policy overload and technological advances provide opportunities rather than curtailment. Universities, working collaboratively and in partnerships, deeply embedded in their localities and regions, but taking a global perspective, will remain crucial to the cultural, economic and community development of the UK and its people.

UCLan is proud of its historical roots, its 200 years of providing a learning institute and a university for Preston, the Lancashire county and the north-west region. Its next stage of growth will be in new models of provision delivery (based on tested traditions in Europe and the United States), new partnership arrangements with further education colleges, maintaining strong links with sister universities in the region, developing the regional economy and continuing to support our students to be technically skilled and apply moral reasoning in their lives and the development of their communities.

NOTES

1. Pope and Phillips, 1995.
2. Pope and Phillips, 1995.
3. Lancashire Strategic Economic Plan, 2014.
4. The Robbins Committee on Higher Education, 1963.
5. Brown, 2011.
6. Berube and Ruth, 2015.
7. Maxwell, 2007.
8. Thorp and Goldstein, 2010.
9. Watson, 2014.
10. Faust, President of Harvard University, 2009.
11. Thomas, 2015.
12. Newman, 1856.
13. Robbins Committee, 1963.
14. Crow and Dabars, 2015.
15. Thorp and Goldstein, 2010.
16. Nowotny et al, 2001.
17. Education Risk Profile PWC, 2015.
18. PWC, 2015.
19. Media FHE Briefing Report 27, 2015.
20. Universities UK, 2015.
21. Hardy, 2013.
22. Hardy, 2013.
23. Kelly, 2015.

REFERENCES

BIS Research Paper Number 171, March 2014, Department for Business, Innovation and Skills.

Centre for Local Economic Strategies (2015) Creating a Good Local Economy, the Role of Anchor Institutions, Express Networks, Manchester.

Kelly, S. (2015) HEPI, Occasional Paper 11, Raising Productivity by Improving Higher Technical Education, Tackling the Level 4 and 5 Conundrum.

Lancashire Strategic Economic Plan, The Growth Deal for the Arc of Prosperity, March 2014, Lancashire Enterprise Partnership.

Media FHE Briefing Report 27 November 2015, Spending Review and Autumn Statement 2015.

Pope, R. and Phillips, K. 1995, University of Central Lancashire, the History of the Development of the Institution since 1828, published by the University of Central Lancashire, Preston.

PWC Higher Education Assurance Services, Current Questions for Higher Education Audit Committees 2015, Published 2015.

PWC Education Sector Risk Profile (2015) PWC London.

QAA 1258 July 15 the Access to Higher Education Diploma, Key Statistics 2013/14 published by the QAA and Access to Higher Education in 2015.

Universities UK, (2015) The Economic Role of UK Universities, Funding Environment for Universities 2015.

Universities UK (2015) Higher Education Facts and Figures 2015.

Universities UK Submission to the 2015 Comprehensive Spending Review, UUK, 2015.

Ward, M. and Hardy, S. (2013) Where next for Local Enterprise Partnerships? Michael Ward and Sally Hardy, The Smith Institute and the Regional Studies Association.

"NOT A WORLD APART"

Universities in Regional Settings

Rick Wylie

Now, more than ever before, education is a categorical imperative. At individual, family, community and regional levels the importance of education cannot be over-stressed. Yet many regional variations in child poverty, social exclusion and a lack of social mobility, are due to poor educational attainment. For many school students, especially those from less advantaged backgrounds, a lack of education denies them access to the digital, knowledge economy in which academic credentials are essential to compete and excel in a high-skill labour market. Moreover, in an era of qualifications inflation and massive competition in the labour market there is a need to possess a wider credentials package to compete successfully for positional goods such as jobs.

This chapter focuses upon educational attainment. It considers a wider role for universities extending into primary and secondary education to work in partnership with schools and school teachers to help address the attainment gap among pupils from less advantaged backgrounds. This engagement could raise the aspirations of pupils and students, especially from less advantaged backgrounds, by promoting and promulgating the idea of a university through engagement with lecturing, research and outreach staff. Through considered, structured contact and engagement this activity could create and sustain the idea of going to university as an attainable ambition throughout an educational career.

This is not to suggest that schools and their staff cannot address the attainment gap. Rather, it suggests how the engagement of university staff from lecturing, research and outreach roles and focusing upon the individual students, could help normalise the idea of a university within the norms of educational beliefs. By adding a new element to the experience of education in primary and secondary schools this could create an attainable, aspirational pathway of progression and self-achievement beyond primary and secondary education which would provide inspiration within primary and secondary education.

Differential attainment in education is an enduring problem in many United Kingdom regions. Despite decades of policy interventions, socio-economic background remains the most significant predictor of attainment in primary and secondary education[1]. Indeed, compelling evidence suggests that, when viewed overall there is a massive attainment gap between pupils from differing demographic backgrounds.

> In 2016, the gap nationally, at the end of secondary school, was still 19.3 months. In fact, disadvantaged pupils fall behind their more affluent peers by around 2 months each year over the course of secondary school.[2]

Since 2007, successive governments have proposed and pursued policies focusing on schools with both Labour, the coalition and Conservative governments pursuing educational policies promising increased social mobility, justice and equality. Gardiner et al[3] purport that these policies are based upon neoliberal principles of marketisation, privatisation, differentiation, decentralisation and competition. In the context of regional development, this activity foregrounds issues of localism and the devolution of power, creating sub-national and sectoral control over academies in an attempt to create success at the institutional and individual pupil levels). However, it has been argued that the shift to academies does not automatically diminish the gap; indeed, it may actually serve to sustain it.

One of the issues facing many pupils from disadvantaged families is their lack of engagement with the 'educational escalator'. Every year, tens of thousands of UK students leave school at 16 with no or very few qualifications. The great majority of low achievers come from disadvantaged backgrounds, though this is, of course, a generalisation and it must be said that many students from these backgrounds do achieve excellent results in primary and secondary schools. However, at the summary level of national statistics, even in the same classes, with the same teachers, books, resources and exercises there is an attainment gap. A child's socio-economic status remains the best predictor of educational attainment, with 27 per cent fewer pupils on free school meals achieving five A*-C GCSEs compared to all other pupils[4].

Much of the influence of a university in its regional setting lies beyond its campus, through its relations with its community. From a regional development standpoint, the role of a university is often equated with its contribution to the regional labour market and to the improvement of communities through improving the educational attainment with the labour market and community levels being the most salient levels of analysis and with pressures to tailor curricula to the requirements of a specific labour market.

Embedded in its locality[5] a university creates a 'learning environment,' develops skills and builds resources for competitiveness and social cohesion. It impacts upon the knowledge economy; engages through its role as an attractor of organisations and families into a region; contributes to the 'institutional thicknesses of a region's economic community of policy and practice; and through its impact upon individual lives, through the demand and supply sides of its local labour market.

For decades all UK universities have engaged with their communities and local schools as part of their wider community role. Science fairs and festivals, school visits, STEM outreach and a host of other engagements have made significant contributions to the perceptions and performance of school pupils across the country. Often unsung and unrecognised, this activity provides a vital linkage between universities and primary and secondary education. In recent years, however, a significant opportunity has emerged to develop this engagement further in the form of the multi academy trust (MAT) and associated educational relationships-initiatives such as teaching schools. It may be that, through engagement with these emerging institutional structures, universities can have an even wider role within education in regions, through a longer-term, coordinated partnership of engagement with staff and students in schools at primary and secondary levels.

Such an approach is consistent with a view of regional development in terms of a network, a 'set of functioning institutions, organisations, funding structures and streams, interactive networks and forums for collaboration, for the pursuit of common economic, social and cultural goals'[6]. In these networks, universities and HEIs are seen as 'anchor institutions' being able to engage with a range of organisations at many levels-it may be that there is a wider network of professional practice involving teaching and research staff in universities and schools working together in wider, regional networks framed within new institutional structures engaged in new relationships at institutional and individual levels.

This chapter has been written at a moment of transition for the University of Central Lancashire's involvement with an academy school in west Cumbria, of which it is a co-owner. West Lakes Academy in Egremont has been a great success in recent years. It has, since its inception and incorporation in 2008, become a school rated 'Outstanding' by OFSTED in early 2017. Formed out of two failing schools, West Lakes Academy was one of the first academies in the country. It is owned by a company limited by guarantee set up by Sellafield Limited, the Nuclear Decommissioning Authority and the University of Central Lancashire (UCLan). This success has been the culmination of a sustained drive by staff, students (and their parents), owners and governors to improve outcomes. Now the goal of achieving an outstanding grade from OFSTED has been realised, and with its achievement of teaching school status and the possible transition to a MAT, thoughts turn to wider contextual issues. In this regard, of special concern is the important issue of the attainment gap between pupils from different socio-economic backgrounds, inclusion and progression between primary and secondary levels of education and wider relationships with the professional communities of practice.

This thinking, and the associated issues and opportunities, has wider relevance for universities, and of special interest are the implications of wider institutional structures which could address one of the key issues facing education in the UK: the difference in attainment between students from more and less advantaged backgrounds. It could be that the idea of going to university would become 'normalised' and students would, from an early age, come to have a relationship, through their school and their teachers, with universities which would not be held as 'a world apart' by students from less advantaged backgrounds. This attainment is so important in a changing labour market, as a House of Commons report[7] argues...

> ...the economy has changed in recent decades; while underachievement in education may once have led to a lifetime of employment in traditional routine manual occupations in factories, the consequence now is more likely to be "NEET" (Not in Education, Employment or Training)[8].

This disadvantage is strongly felt by those in this position colouring their worldview and beliefs, and shaping their aspirations. A study by the Prince's Trust of a sample of over two thousand 16 to 24 year-olds on an online poll conducted by YouGov in spring 2011 found that...

- More than one in five of those from deprived homes (22 per cent) believe that 'few' or 'none' of their goals in life are achievable, compared to just five per cent of those from affluent families
- More than one in four young people growing up in poverty (26 per cent) believe that 'few' or 'none' of their career goals are

achievable, compared to just seven per cent of those from wealthy families

- One in four young people from poor homes (26 per cent) feel that 'people like them don't succeed in life'
- Almost a quarter from deprived homes (24 per cent) believe they will "end up on benefits for at least part of their life" and more than one in five feel they will end up in a 'dead-end job'
- Around one in six young people from poor homes (16 per cent) say their family and friends have made fun of them when they talk about finding a good job[9].

One of the key issues underlying this differential attainment crisis is aspirations, a concept which captures the desires and ambitions young people hold about their futures which shape their engagement in the present. Essentially, a desire to achieve something high in the future has implications to shape people's actions in the present, but this requires inspiration in the present and here, it is argued, social setting and socialisation are key influences upon individuals.

Essentially, aspirations may be defined in this context as '…a student's ability to identify and set goals for the future, while being inspired in the present to work towards those goals.'[10] Of particular relevance to this chapter is the notion that there are two elements to aspirations – inspiration and ambition.

- "Inspiration reflects that an activity is exciting and enjoyable to the individual and the awareness of being fully and richly involved in life here and now. It is depicted by an individual who becomes involved in an activity for its intrinsic value and enjoyment. An individual with a high level of inspiration is one who believes an activity is useful and enjoyable.
- Ambitions represent the perception that an activity is important as a means to future goals. It reflects individuals' perceptions that it is both possible and desirable to think in future terms and to plan for the future."[11]

In recent years, there has been a significant level of policy interest in raising aspirations to address child poverty. As Kintrea[12] found, aspirations are often lowest in white, council-built neighbourhoods in former industrial areas. Crucially, aspirations may change, influenced by the social context within which individuals live and with which they come to identify over time. It may be that lower aspirations are an informed and rational response to specific cultural and social contexts. They may be strongly influenced by what Festinger[13] termed 'social comparison', an influential dynamic which, it is argued,[14] is especially strong in school classroom settings. A recent report by DCSF argued...

> Children living in deprived communities face a cultural barrier which is in many ways a bigger barrier (to success) than material poverty. It is a cultural barrier of low aspirations and scepticism about education, the feeling that education is by and for other people, and likely to let one down[15].

Thus in the areas of most need individuals may have poor frames of social, educational and economic reference. From a regional policy standpoint, these factors can lead to the double bind of self-perpetuating poverty and declining social mobility, which is evident in many communities.

Other data reveals the importance of social setting and context – essentially cultural standards in social settings strongly influence individual expectations and performance. In 2009 a UK government white paper on social mobility identified a key role for communities in shaping young people's attitudes to education and employment. The premise of the white paper was that: 'Growing up in a strong positive community encourages us to set our sights high and helps us to develop the resilience to overcome adversity and achieve our goals'[16]. In contrast: 'In some deprived communities stable populations and close knit networks combine with a sense of isolation from broader social and economic opportunities. This can limit young people's horizons and aspirations for the future'[17]

Clearly, context shapes aspirations, which can, in turn, drive an individual towards achievement. Our brief insight into aspirations reveals its nature as having an impact in both inspiration and ambition, and sustained engagement with a university may make a significant and substantive contribution to educational attainment, especially among those whose family background and social setting does not include an experience involving the idea, or experience, of a university.

BUT WHAT CAN UNIVERSITIES DO?

In an examination of schools' links with higher education Tough and her colleagues argued:

> It is clear that there could be large benefits to pupils, teachers and universities from longer-term programmes with pupils in schools rather than ad-hoc projects which, although often repeated each year, are not repeatedly engaging the same pupils. One way of achieving this is through long-term structural engagement such as a university supporting an academy or trust, but it is clear that this level and model of engagement would not be possible for all schools. Schools and colleges also felt that structural engagement through HE representation on the school or college governing body did not have much impact in terms of tangible benefits to pupils around access to HE links[18].

Two issues emerge from this analysis. Firstly, that longer-term engagement is necessary to achieve real benefit; and secondly, that university or HE representation should, to achieve real benefit among pupils, occur at a more operational and less strategic level. This important issue of levels of engagement was made recently by the principal and CEO of a successful academy, who felt that universities may find it more fruitful, and flexible, to engage within the framework of a Teaching School structure at a more operational level[19].

Engagement in MATs and associated initiatives, like teaching schools, may provide opportunities to engage the higher education sector in schools and generate meaningful, sustained engagement.

A MAT is, of course, an initiative established to undertake strategic collaboration to improve and maintain high educational standards across a number of schools within the context of a single entity with a group of schools forming a single (multi academy) trust which has overarching responsibility for their governance.

It may be that a MAT structure could create an institutional framework for engaging staff from primary, secondary and higher education institutions within an inter-institutional framework to normalise the idea of a university. Clearly, a multi-academy trust provides a greater institutional breadth and scale for engagement between members of institutions. Engagement in the governance of the institution creating approved organisational space enables contact to be regularised and routinised across appropriate levels involving practitioners, pupils and (institutional) policy levels.

The impact of embedded interactions at the operational level between institutions is revealed by three case studies in Adonis: 'Firstly, in Nottingham, the university opened William Samworth Academy and commenting upon this institution, one of Nottingham's pro vice-chancellors noted that "We set out to create a sense that a university is a very normal thing, not a world apart...'[20]. Commenting on the breadth and depth of the relationship, Adonis noted,

> ...the university provides more than governors and governance: its lecturers, students and support staff being part of the life of the school. All new pupils go on a "transition day" at the university. The academy has a sixth form and Nottingham's students act as mentors ('the conversations don't always stay on topic', as one student puts it). The university also supports the academy through apprenticeships and work placements. More than 20 academy staff are undertaking masters and doctoral degrees at the university. A team from the university... with two playwrights and a group of local residents, making a series of plays about Bilborough past, present and future.[21]

Secondly, in Bristol the engagement of the local university in an academy 'helped hugely in raising aspirations among staff and students' said a principal sponsor of the academy which was developed in partnership with the University of the West of England. He went on: 'Staying-on rates after GCSE have increased dramatically compared to its predecessor failing comprehensive, and the number of students going on to university has trebled since the start of the academy.'[22]

In London, Adonis noted that UCL (one of Britain's leading research universities) was establishing an academy in its home Borough of Camden in London. This integration between university and academy was leading to 'a curriculum developed in exciting ways informed by the latest research', and university mentors 'to provide role models, classroom assistants, and sources of informal advice and guidance to students'. These cases reveal the potential of engagement between a university at two levels. Institutional engagement to set the framework and individual staff level to work with and within the academy reflecting the provost's view that 'A modern university should not be divorced from secondary education in its own locality'[23].

These examples reveal the potential of an embedded university working in a regional, place setting engaged with a wider institutional structure and how the university could impact upon the aspirations and expectations of students from all backgrounds working through the elements of a wider institution. In this wider institutional arrangement, professional practice and personal engagement would occur across a wider 'new' institution, a discursive institution engaging wider communities of practice. A key element of this engagement would involve a programme of engagement with individual pupils to shape and support their aspirations and make their expectations realistic and achievable.

Working within the framework of a MAT involving primary and secondary schools a university could work with teaching staff and have a positive impact on pupils (and staff), especially over the key transition between primary and secondary education. Within the greater scale of a MAT this could give a more appropriate scale of resource utilisation and allow a longer duration of effect extending over almost a decade of schooling in some cases.

From this overview of activities, two key points have emerged. Firstly, that interventions need to be sustained over the long term to have a significant and enduring impact upon pupils' aspirations (and consequent attainment). And, secondly, that the architecture of institutional engagement needs to encompass both the strategic governance and operational practice embedded within a collaborative structure focused upon the individual student and their wider opportunities beyond the local community and local labour market. What is being proposed here is beyond one-off outreach activities and short-term projects. Rather, it would involve staff from schools and universities working collaboratively in inter-institutional structures at an operational level in a long-term partnership collaborating in their complementary areas of professional practice in primary, secondary and higher education. This programme would provide students with innovative engagement focused upon the student experience and helping them set goals for their future and inspiring them to work towards them.

SUMMARY AND CONCLUSION

This chapter has introduced some ideas about a role of universities in primary and secondary education, which have emerged out of experience with successful academies and university collaborations and more detailed insights from engagement in a single academy trust in Cumbria. No longer elite institutions, the 'massification' and 'marketisation' of universities has resulted in universities' participation in many spheres of society addressing local labour markets and the needs of industry and offering courses tailored and targeted at the needs of the labour market. What has been discussed in this chapter is a further, systematic extension of the university into primary and secondary education where it would aim to provide a long-term programme of educational innovation, individual inspiration working in partnership within the educational fabric of schools, within the scope of a university's teaching, research and knowledge-transfer activities.

MAT[24] structures and associated programmes, such as teaching schools, could be appropriate vehicles for a university to engage, at institutional and individual levels, with staff and students in primary and secondary schools. This engagement could promote the idea of a university as an accessible, achievable ambition especially for pupils and students from less advantaged backgrounds – raising aspirations through long-term engagements throughout primary and secondary education.

It is not being suggested that universities can do the educational job of colleagues in primary and secondary schools any better. What is being proposed here is a partnership collaboration through a considered programme of interaction at both individual and institutional levels between pupils and practitioners set within long-term institutional frameworks. What is proposed here is not a one-off initiative, but a long-term programme embedded in institutional agreements and professional practice and personal relationships.

Much of the literature on the regional role of a university stresses its regional-level impact in respect of workforce, but there is a less appreciated aspect to a university's wider, social impact in regions. For decades most universities have engaged in outreach with schools and this has undoubtedly contributed to raising aspirations among school pupils. However, what is stressed in effective examples of engagement is longer-term contact with pupils and that requires a wider institutional framework. The neoliberal educational policies adopted in primary and secondary education by successive administrations over almost two decades are leading to more localised and devolved arrangements in the governance of schools. These developments have created an opportunity for a wider engagement between universities, schools and pupils through the establishment of a

MAT and the strategic and systematic engagement of a higher education institution within one inspiring and motivating pupils from all backgrounds and making higher education appear less of a 'world apart' from the school and local community experience.

NOTES

1. Gardiner, 2017.
2. Andrews et al, 2017.
3. Gardiner, 2017.
4. DfE, 2011.
5. Boucher et al 2003, page 887.
6. Hotta, 2000 in Boucher et al, 2003.
7. House of Commons report, 2014.
8. House of Commons report, 2014.
9. Prince's Trust, 2011.
10. Quaglia and Cobb, 1996.
11. Quaglia and Cobb, 1996, page 130.
12. Kintrea, 2009.
13. Festinger, 1954.
14. Levine et al, 1983.
15. DCSF, 2008, page 2, cited in Kintrea, 2009, page 1.
16. Cabinet Office, 2009, cited in Kintrea, 2009.
17. Cabinet Office, 2009, cited in Kintrea 2009.
18. Tough et al, 2008.
19. Johnston, 2017.
20. Adonis 2012, page 170.
21. Adonis 2012, page 170.
22. Adonis 2012, page 171.
23. Malcolm Grant, provost of UCL Cited in Adonis 2012, pages 171–2.
24. The Department for Education defines MATs as: 'Multi-academy trusts usually run more than one academy. The MAT has a single set of articles and therefore is a single legal entity accountable for a number of academies. The trust enters into a Master Funding Agreement (MFA) with the Secretary of State, and into Supplemental Funding Agreements (SFA) for each academy it operates.'

REFERENCES

Adonis, A. (2012) Education, Education, Education: Reforming England's Schools. London, Biteback Publishing.

Andrews, J. Robinson, D. and Jo Hutchinson (2017) Closing the Gap? Trends in Educational Attainment and Disadvantage. Education Policy Institute.

Armstrong, P. (2015) Effective School Partnerships and Collaboration for School Improvement: a Review of the Evidence. Research report, Department for Education.

Boucher, G. Conway, C. and Van Der Meer, E. (2003) Tiers of Engagement by Universities in their Region's Development. *Regional Studies*, Vol. 37.9, Pages 887–897, 2003.

Cabinet Office (2009) New Opportunities: Fair Chances for the Future (Social Mobility White Paper), Cm7533.

Festinger, L. (1954) A theory of social comparison Processes. Human Relations Vol. 7 Pages 117–140. Cited in in Levine, J. M., Ed. and Wang, M. C., Ed. (1983) Teacher and Student Perception: Implications for Learning. Hillsdale, N.J., Lawrence Erlbaum Associates, Inc. Pages 29–55.

Gardiner, J. (2017) Social Class and Educational Achievement in Modern England: How Has the Coalition Government's Academies Programme Impacted the Social Class Achievement Gap? https://www.researchgate.net/publication/318661282_Social_Class_and_Educational_Achievement_in_Modern_England_How_Has_the_Coalition_Government's_Academies_Programme_Impacted_the_Social_Class_Achievement_Gap [accessed Oct 18 2017].

House of Commons Education Committee (2014) Underachievement in Education by White Working Class Children. London, HMSO HC142.

House of Commons Education Committee (2017) Multi-academy trusts: Seventh Report of Session 2016–17. Report, together with formal minutes relating to the report. House of Commons Education Committee HC 204.

Johnston, Jonathan, Principal of West Lakes Academy, personal communication dated 12 September 2017.

Kintrea, Keith. (2017). Aspirations, Attainment and Social Mobility in Disadvantaged Areas. European Network for Housing Research, Prague, June 2009.

Quaglia, J. and Cobb, Casey, D. (1996) Toward a Theory of Student Aspirations Journal of Research in Rural Education Vol. 12 No. 3. Pages 127–132.

The Prince's Trust (2011) Broke, not Broken: Tackling Youth Poverty and the Aspiration Gap.

Tough, S. Sasis, A. and Geoff Whitty (2008) Productive Partnerships? An examination of schools' links with higher education A report on research carried out for the Sutton Trust. Institute of Education, University of London.

ENTREPRENEURIAL UNIVERSITIES IN A REGIONAL CONTEXT

John Lonsdale

INTRODUCTION

This chapter considers entrepreneurial universities in a regional context. Some measures of entrepreneurship favour wealthy institutions and these have featured prominently in the literature. By attracting large volumes of research income and drawing upon rich resources they can translate this into a high number of start-ups and spin-outs. However, these institutions are very much in the minority, but all is not lost for other universities with fewer existing resources. Enterprising and entrepreneurial approaches can make a significant difference to not only the institution, but to the student base and relations with stakeholders in the region and beyond.

This chapter surveys some key underpinning literature in this area, focusing on how entrepreneurial approaches in universities can produce a wide range of benefits, academically, for students and for regional economies. The approach goes beyond the narrow measure of spin out creation and considers how the context of the university will influence its approach.

Universities are well placed to take advantage of existing networks, create new networks and to deploy the immense social capital that they possess. Acknowledgment is given to the tensions of academic workloads and identity as serious concerns that need to be considered in any strategy.

Each needs to find its own way – while broad principles are generalisable, the outcomes will be a function of resources and networks built by the universities. These contextual resources in some way constrain universities, but can also be the basis for distinctive development and differentiation from other instructions.

An example of this approach as undertaken at the University of Central Lancashire (UCLan), a large enterprising university in the north-west of England, is provided.

THE ENTREPRENEURIAL UNIVERSITY – AN OVERVIEW

While surveys of the literature[1] suggest that academic entrepreneurship as a field of scholarly study is relatively new; in fact the concept of entrepreneurial universities has a much longer history. There is a fertile body of literature looking at the idea of the entrepreneurial university.

Drucker[2] writes 'no better text for a history of entrepreneurship could be found than the creation and development of the modern university' and cites the creation of the University of Berlin by Humboldt in 1809 as a key example, which was then picked up in the United States some 60 years later. Humboldt's objectives were to take intellectual and scientific leadership away from the French and capture the energies released by the French Revolution, and so the idea of university activities being used for economic advantage is nothing new.

In long-term studies of university transformation, Clark[3] identified five elements that enable that transformation. These are: a strengthened steering core with strength to set an independent course; the expanded development periphery which includes cross-discipline projects and TTOs; a diversified funding base; a stimulated academic heartland; and an integrated entrepreneurial culture. These elements suggest that for universities to be truly entrepreneurial, coordinated action is needed throughout the organisation to enact the five elements – they are unlikely to come about by chance, and therefore support at government and university board level is required.

In a study of 15 UK universities, Martin and Turner[4] consider the tensions created by trying to create entrepreneurial universities, especially when commercial missions are placed on top of a traditionally focused organisation. Recounting the experiences of staff, 'participants felt there were simultaneously two levels of reality – the voiced mission statement ... and the signaled purposes which emphasises the need to bring in money and raise profiles'[5]. Other observations included different views as to what their roles were and what commercialisation meant, doubts about personal capability to do such work and the lack of practical curriculum. The findings highlighted the need for policymakers to understand the heterogeneity of the HIE base and to address organisational cultures related to third mission activities in their organisation[6].

Themes of change and adaptability come out of the literature. Davies[7] suggests that entrepreneurial universities are those with commercial and financial awareness; they are more than just adaptable. While many organisations show signs of responsiveness and adaptability to their new situation, this is arguably not the same as entrepreneurial behaviour. Entrepreneurial universities reach out, extending their own boundaries and are players in shaping their own environment.

ACADEMIC ENTREPRENEURS

Universities host and develop a wide range of entrepreneurs and intrapreneurs. This raises two questions: the first as to what we consider an entrepreneur to be like and do, and the second the implications of being entrepreneurial in large organisations like universities.

There are many and varied definitions of entrepreneurship. Schumpeter[8] describes an entrepreneur as a person who is willing and able to convert a new idea or invention into a successful innovation. Druilhe and Garnsey[9] define entrepreneurship as 'the pursuit of opportunity and the mobilisation of resources to deliver value and capture returns'. Shattock[10] offers a brief but provoking definition of entrepreneurship in an academic context as 'extending the boundaries of the university'. This idea of boundary pushing is reflected in Clark[11]:

> The new understanding is that entrepreneurship is not a personality type, nor is it a stage in the life cycle of an organisation. Rather, it is a way of managing, where one pursues opportunities beyond means that are currently available.

Other definitions focus more on venture or business creation. Johnson[12] defines entrepreneurship as capturing ideas, converting them into products and services, building a venture to take them to market. Shane et al[13] describe entrepreneurship as a process by which opportunities to create future goods and services are discovered, evaluated and exploited. This is described as a creative process and does imply the creation of a company.

For universities, the focus on venture creation is arguably too narrow and unhelpful. Brenkert[14] suggests that being an entrepreneur is not about owning a business, but about the behaviours employed by the entrepreneur. Brenkert assesses various definitions of entrepreneurship and proposes that it has a dual nature: 'the project to be realised and the organisation or organisational efforts to realise it'. Brenkert's work raises many interesting questions related to the nature of entrepreneurship and possible conflict in terms of values and behavioural cultures of academics. Are academia and entrepreneurship compatible and are there aspects of universities that should not be 'polluted' by commercialisation?

In an exploration of innovation and entrepreneurship, Johnson[15] defines an entrepreneur as an individual who takes agency and initiative, manages risk, is persistent and makes things happen. Corporate entrepreneurship is defined as having three main forms:

intrapreneurship, dispersed entrepreneurship and corporate venturing. This definition is useful in placing academic entrepreneurs in a category of intrapreneurship, with its own particular literature and examples of success.

Even research can be considered to be inherently entrepreneurial. It can be argued that because research groups form and compete for funds, they have the characteristics of early stage firms, even before they engage in overtly entrepreneurial activities. Entrepreneurial universities can act like a large incubator, with a large turnover of human capital (students), with which to provide ideas (Etzkowitz[16]). Controversies regarding academic entrepreneurship, include the need for guidelines and legitimacy for the activity and the existence and coexistence of apparently antithetical norms and orientations.

These definitions and distinctions show that there is plenty of scope for academics to be entrepreneurial within the organisational framework of the university. Business creation is not always required, and the scope for building opportunities could occur in any field. With the growth in social enterprises, there is also clarity that the rationale for entrepreneurial activity is not just related income generation, but to achieving particular social goals, though in practice most commercial projects should also generate academic and ancillary social benefits (e.g. student work opportunities) as well.

ROLE OF THE UNIVERSITY

With multiple stakeholders, debate and discussion about the purpose and role of universities has been ongoing for as long as they have existed. It is clear that universities now go beyond Newman's 'universal school of learning' and further into the realms of economic development and application of knowledge. Shattock[17] notes that the boundaries of universities are extending: the exploitation of knowledge and regional development roles creates a challenge for university managers. These roles of universities extend to enhancing the democratisation of knowledge (Delanty[18]), playing an enhanced role in technological development (Etzkowitz et al.[19]), and 'development of a third role performed by universities in animating regional economic, social and civic development' (Warren et al)[20].

In Europe, the main types are the Humboldtian model typical of Germany, the Napoleonic model typical of France and Spain, the Nordic model typical of Sweden and Finland, the Anglo-Saxon model typical of the United Kingdom and much of the US, and the central and eastern European model typical of Poland and Russia. Koivula and Rinne[21] note that, although the ties of the state may be looser in the Anglo-Saxon model than in other models, this is more than compensated for by market forces; autonomy is being seen to be reduced by the responsibilities given to it in society and by government[22]. They suggest that 'the central challenges for the modern university stem from its increased function, massification, shortage of public funding and rapid changes in its operational environment'[23].

Some, for example Delanty[24], argue that universities should be key actors in the public sphere and enhance the democratisation of knowledge and that generally, through the middles ages to modern society, universities have managed to keep a separation from social struggles. This is somewhat contentious, as access to universities has historically tended to be a function of ability to pay, as has access to good primary and secondary education, both of which tend to be socially or economically defined, rather than defined by any notion of democratic fairness. Other key trends include the diverse places in which knowledge is now created, from think-tanks and companies to consultancies, reducing the monopoly claims of universities with respect to knowledge creation[25].

More recently, internet access, online resources and the availability of information are forcing institutions to think about the value of what they provide in terms of learning experience and opportunities to learn through application of knowledge. Abeles[26] proposes that technology fundamentally changes the role of academia and the distribution of knowledge. In his essay on the development of education and the impact of the internet, the idea that you cannot unscramble eggs is used to suggest the irreversibility of technology and commercialism. He argues that a new market of open competition is evident, with ivory tower academics forced into the open on a new playing field. If this is true, universities will find themselves drawn into markets, where enterprise and entrepreneurship will be a heightened requirement for survival.

Thus, definitions of universities as creators and disseminators of knowledge and producers of knowledgeable people seem too narrow. They have the means to be more prominent actors in society and the economy, actively shaping their environment. Universities play an enhanced role in technological development and governments encourage this as an economic development strategy. In the UK, a critical moment occurred in 1985, when the intellectual property right functions of the state agency British Technology Group were devolved to universities, setting the scene for entrepreneurial universities (Etzkowitz et al[27]). The authors describe entrepreneurial development across the world as being a common and prevalent trend, but note that the precise forms, speed and implementation vary greatly with local conditions. The broader literature concurs with this, with American universities in particular being ahead in entrepreneurial development.

This somewhat late adoption of intellectual property and its development to commercialisation is perhaps at the root of stereotypes and accusations that UK universities are great at coming up with ideas which other countries then make money from.

UNIVERSITY-INDUSTRY LINKAGES

University-industry linkages and their associated issues are not a new phenomenon. For example, Bowie[28] cites examples from the 1920s: the Wisconsin Alumni Research Foundation and its commercialisation of Vitamin D irradiation processes and commercialisation of 43 other inventions over the following 50 years; and MIT, which was funded by AT&T and GE from around 1915. Both became embroiled in the patent management issues, business ethics debates, funding issues and teaching autonomy-related discussions, which appear in more recent literature.

In a summary of the EUERK study of European Union universities, 1994–2004, Shattock[29] notes that universities have increased their commitment to knowledge transfer enormously. He argues that autonomy of the institution is an important precursor to academic entrepreneurship in universities, but that entrepreneurship might conform to a certain pattern. Another observation was that 'entrepreneurialism in a university setting is about generating activities, which extend a university's traditional boundaries', again taking the notion that application and use of knowledge is critical in the wider remit of universities.

Technology transfer offices (TTOs) play a key role in university-industry links. For example, Siegel et al[30] argue that the efficiency of university linkages can be affected by organisational factors, such as staffing, efficient processes and the ability of the TTOs to act in a boundary-spanning way – a bridge between firms and scientists. Siegel et al[31] highlight the need to attract institutional entrepreneurs into TTOs to enable the commercialisation of ideas. Drawing upon the earlier discussion of multiple logics in this literature review, one can imagine that academics with the ambidexterity to handle the translation across the logics would be well suited to the TTO role.

Clear policies are also key to managing the effects of university research relationships and academic capitalism. For example, a US study of agricultural biotech collaborations across nine universities, concluded that there is a complex set of effects in play, due to the interactions between actors and the IP policies adopted. The university scientists believe that communication is restricted if commercial IP restrictions are used. They believe that ideally IP policies should shield them from opportunistic behaviour, while at the same time promoting industry collaboration (Welsh et al).[32]

REGIONAL CONTEXT IS IMPORTANT

Although much of the literature considers the university or the academic, the university is not a stand-alone body. Forces act upon it and are critical in any analysis. Fairweather[33] discusses the notion of generalisability, by which they mean that just because something works somewhere it will not necessarily work everywhere. There is a danger that people will follow suit in trying to emulate successful examples, but without due consideration for the resources, networks and general environment that made the success work. The literature on universities certainly suggests this is true; the varied university models in each country, local legislation and cultural aspects mean that due consideration of context is required before reusing ideas or results from research.

Wright et al[34], researching academic entrepreneurship in Europe and the conditions for spin-out companies, identified that for the UK, key elements affecting the rate of spin-outs will be researchers status, business training for academics, incubators and other business support and financing. On the same theme, but looking at spin-out performance, Doutriaux[35] summarises studies of firms with and without university ties, in service and manufacturing categories. A negative correlation was discovered between spin-out performance and closeness to the university, for example, if the academics involved retained an academic post. Sales and employment are lower on average than for non-affiliated firms. This is somewhat counterintuitive to ideas that close university linkages would give advantages, but according to Doutriaux may be related to the academic entrepreneur themselves and their commitment to the new venture.

The impact of government intervention is explored by Clarysse et al[36]. They examine the use of research and development subsidies and consider to what degree market failure discourages research and development. They explore ideas of input additionality (the incentivisation of companies to do extra R&D) versus output additionality (was produced for the extra spend). In addition, they scrutinise behavioural additionality (what changes in personal or organisational behaviour during or after a project).

From these ideas we can see that entrepreneurial condition will vary, from country to country, from region to region depending on government policy and economic conditions. The effects of institutional models come into play, with the British-Anglo Saxon model seemingly quite well suited to industrial collaboration but weak in areas. Specific geographical constraints will apply in terms of the number of organisations available to interact with and the environment. Institutional policies, discussed later in more detail, will determine the capacity of the university to act with the environment effectively.

CHALLENGES FACING AN ENTREPRENEURIAL UNIVERSITY

While the environmental context shapes the activity of entrepreneurial universities, there is a wide range of organisational challenges, not least in the demands of academic careers, the importance of academic identity and the subsequent view of what constitutes legitimate academic work. Legitimacy describes the fit with the culture, norms and goals of the organisation. In studies investigating the influence of legitimacy human and social capital in start-ups created by university employees, legitimacy was not found be a factor affecting start-ups. While knowledge of starting up helps, a Swedish study by Karlsson and Wigren[37] found more educated, senior, older academics were less likely to create start-ups. Social capital indicators showed a positive correlation, with participation in product development, contract research or external linked projects all indicating an increased likelihood of initiating a start-up. The recommendations are that universities wanting to promote this activity should promote industry linkages and should also consider getting early stage career researchers involved in this activity at any early stage.

Some researchers go beyond the observation of the academic and explore the motivations in more detail. Jain et al[38] discuss the micro-foundations and micro-mechanisms of the motivation process, in particular the individual level transactions that affect academic entrepreneurship, in particular the role of the main actor – the university scientist. This US study looks at the willingness of academics to modify their behaviour to the new role of entrepreneur and suggests there is a hybrid mentality at play. Sense-making and role-defining dimensions for academics and others are seen as important. Looking at the social-psychological factors, George et al[39] discuss entrepreneurial identity and invention disclosure behaviour. The presentation discusses the reasons why scientists become entrepreneurs (both economic and non-economic reasons) and the multiple identity issues presented (academic, teacher and entrepreneur).

Colyvas[40] describes a longitudinal study of the Stanford University life sciences technology transfer programme, 1968–1992. Institutional logics or norms which bound acceptable behaviour are described, along with the logic and the politics of collaborations[41]. A series of models is offered including: 'teamwork', where many members of the lab collaborated and were supported by commercial experts; 'science is not for profit', where the academics were loath to seek sole credit for patents and did not see the patents as useful to the university; 'non faculty career', which describes a high level of industry engagement; and 'contribution matters', where academics start to see the value of what they do, demand compensation for it and use patents to protect against exploitation. The author describes how norms changed over time[42]. Patents were initially used as a way to protect research and then the role of commercialisation gradually became incorporated into the university mission and accepted.

Considering the commercialisation of university research, Ambos et al[43] look at the tensions on research organisations and propose the idea of ambidexterity – doing one thing while continuing to do another. Ambos et al. show that the tension between academic and commercial activities is more pronounced at researcher level, rather than higher institutional level – 'the people who deliver commercial outcomes tend to be rather different to those who are accustomed to producing academic outcomes'[44]. In their UK-based study, they observe that universities are not required to switch from one activity to another – they are required to do both. They found that TTOs may signal an intention to commercialise, but the breadth of support and experience in the TTOs are not significant predictors of commercial outcomes[45]. At an individual level, high embeddedness of researchers is a negative factor, with younger researchers showing more signs of commercial activity. Conversely and simultaneously, the scientific excellence of principal investigators has the opposite effect, creating a nuanced continuum. Young, less senior and highly cited researchers are likely to have highest commercial output. Thus, options for increasing commercial outputs include developing TTOs and other support mechanisms; legitimising commercial outputs as an activity; seeking and promoting ambidextrous high achievers to act as role models, and incentivising more embedded researchers who are locked in academic research trajectories.

Hence, universities seeking to be truly entrepreneurial face a wide range of challenges, to reconcile the rules, values and norms of academia with the rules, values and norms of external organisations. Motivations, career stages and desired outcomes need to be carefully thought through. Then adequate support needs to be put in place to enable it.

CASE STUDY: AN ANALYSIS OF FACTORS THAT CONTRIBUTE TO THE ENTREPRENEURIAL UNIVERSITY

As well as the more general contextual elements that contribute towards an enterprising or entrepreneurial university, there are many that are relevant to academics themselves, not only external to the university but within the ecosystem of the university. In a survey of UCLan academics, opinions were sought against a series of

Table 4.1   Survey Questionnaire Results for UCLan Academics

Staff Questionnaire	Overall Response
I know what the latest trends are in my subject field	Strongly Agree
I enjoy getting involved in the external activities related to my subject	Strongly Agree
I sometimes have ideas about new projects and take them to colleagues	Strongly Agree
I have a good network of contacts outside the University	Strongly Agree
I feel comfortable doing work outside the University	Strongly Agree
Non-teaching or research activity will be good for my career	Strongly Agree
I find it easy to find and talk to people in my field about ideas I have	Strongly Agree
I feel confident about making predictions about trends in my field	Strongly Agree
Opportunities come my way through my contacts	Strongly Agree
Doing enterprising work will help my research and teaching	Strongly Agree
Knowledge transfer is as important as teaching and research	Strongly Agree
I have successfully taken an idea forward that became a project, course or service	Strongly Agree
I have a good network of contacts in the University	Strongly Agree
I am a member of subject interest groups (committees, societies, institutes) outside the University	Strongly Agree
I like taking on new projects, even if they might fail	Strongly Agree
The University trusts me to get on with my dealings outside the University	Strongly Agree
Being at the University offers me a chance to develop my own projects and ideas	Strongly Agree
The University is an innovative organisation	Strongly Agree
I represent the University in my subject area in committees and other groups	Agree
I feel able to act when I have a good idea	Agree
It is easy for me to link teaching, research and enterprising work together so that they benefit each other	Agree
We often discuss new ideas and projects in our school	Agree
I deal with external clients on a regular basis	Agree
I am happy discussing commercial matters with clients	Agree

(cont. . .)

Table 4.1   Survey Questionnaire Results for UCLan Academics (*continued*)

Staff Questionnaire	*Overall Response*
My colleagues support me when I am doing work which is not teaching or research	Agree
I know what other people in the University do that relates to my field	Agree
My line manager supports me when I am doing work which is not teaching or research	Agree
I am a member of subject interest groups in the University	No clear consensus
I know where to go to get help if I want to develop a commercial project such as CPD, consultancy or a new product	No clear consensus
The University supports me in non teaching and research work	No clear consensus
School plans have a guiding effect on my work	No clear consensus
I use personal appraisals to negotiate time and resource for new projects	No clear consensus
I am able to get new ideas raised and considered at school committees	No clear consensus
I am able to negotiate or haggle for resources and time when I need it	No clear consensus
My appraisal helps me to progress my ideas	No clear consensus
The University's strategies are helpful when coming up with ideas and developing projects	Disagree
I have been able access commercial training when required	Disagree
I know how commercial projects are set up and developed in the University	Disagree
I know that if my project failed I would be supported by the University	Disagree
Early stage academics get good KT experience at the University	Disagree
I am able to access the funding I need to develop new ideas I have	Strongly disagree
I get adequate reward (e.g. recognition or money) for ideas I come up with	Strongly disagree
I am able to manage my work balance of teaching, research and KT easily	Strongly disagree

Factors that contribute towards an entrepreneurial university (Lonsdale, 2013) questions that were derived from a model of entrepreneurship based on actor network theory. The underlying reasoning was that enterprising universities build on their network resources, assembling (the actors) in specific combinations through means of negotiation, acknowledging issues such as power structures and risk appetites within the institution.

While the approach and questions can be used in most institutions, the results summarised here are specific to UCLan, a university with a long history, over 32,000 students and over 1,000 academic staff. The questions reflect the linkages between academics, their subject areas, colleagues and fellow academics as well as outside actors such as companies and collaborators.

From UCLan's point of view the results were both encouraging and also signalled areas to focus upon if more engagement of staff was to be possible. A key finding was that staff do believe that entrepreneurial or commercial work is a legitimate activity and are looking for opportunities to get involved. Because of the contact of the university, a high number of staff have good networks in either industry or the public sector, often gained from early careers in professional practice.

The challenges arise in three key areas: funding for new ideas; challenges with balancing work load and freeing up time from teaching; and being rewarded for the work, through career progression, monetary or other non-monetary mechanisms.

THE IMPLICATIONS FOR STRATEGY

These findings have been taken into account in UCLan's strategies going forward. For example, new career routes and criteria have been implemented, work load models revised and funding put in place to support ideas to progress. Professional support has been bolstered to keep commercial work away from academic colleagues where possible to allow them to concentrate on the innovative work and associated academic activity.

CONCLUSIONS

For entrepreneurial universities it can be argued that context, both in the external environment and the specific resources (including staff students and wider stakeholders), will shape activity, but that is not to say that there not common approaches that universities can take. By examining the regional socio-economic context and also taking stock of the staff and students within the institution, new strategies and plans delivering a wide range of academic, financial and wider social benefits can be constructed.

NOTES

1. Rothaermel et al, 2007.
2. Drucker 2007, page 21.
3. Clark 1998, page 4.
4. Martin and Turner, 2010.
5. Martin and Turner, 2009, page 17.
6. Martin and Turner, 2009, page 19.
7. Davies 2001, pages 28–29.
8. Schumpeter, 1950.
9. Druilhe and Garnsey, 2004.
10. Shattock, 2009, page 205.
11. Clark, 2001, page 16.
12. Johnson, 2001a.
13. Shane et al, 2003, page 259.
14. Brenkert, 2009, page 450.
15. Johnson, 2001a, page 137.
16. Etzkowitz 2003, page 112.
17. Shattock, 2010, page 127.
18. Delanty, 2001, page 9.
19. Etzkowitz et al., 2000, page 319.
20. Warren et al, 2010.
21. Koivula and Rinne, 2006, page 2.
22. Koivula and Rinne, 2006, page 6.
23. Koivula and Rinne, 2006, page 7.
24. Delanty, 2001, page 9.
25. Delanty, 2001, page 103.

26. Abeles, 2001.
27. Etzkowitz et al, 2000, page 319.
28. Bowie, 1994, pages 5–13.
29. Shattock, 2009, pages 200–206.
30. Siegel et al, 2003, page 45.
31. Siegel et al, 2007, page 497.
32. Welsh et al, 2008.
33. Fairweather, 1988, page 86.
34. Wright et al, 2007, page 49.
35. Doutriaux, 1987, page 296.
36. Clarysse et al, 2009.
37. Karlsson and Wigren, 2010.
38. Jain et al, 2009, page 927.
39. George et al, 2005.
40. Colyvas, 2007.
41. Colyvas, 2007, page 458.
42. Colyvas, 2007, page 474.
43. Ambos et al, 2008.
44. Ambos et al, 2008, page 1424.
45. Ambos et al, 2008, page 1442.

REFERENCES

Abeles, T. P. 2001. You Can't Unscramble Eggs. On the Horizon, 9(1), 2–4.

Ambos, T. C., Mäkel, K., Birkinshaw, J. and D'Este, P. 2008. When Does University Research Get Commercialized? Creating Ambidexterity in Research Institutions. Journal of Management Studies, 45(8), 1424–1447.

Bowie, N. E. 1994. University-business partnerships: an assessment, Lanham, MD; London: Rowman & Littlefield.

Clark, B. R. 1998. Creating entrepreneurial universities: organizational pathways of transformation, New York; Oxford: Pergamon.

Clark, B. R. 2001. The Entrepreneurial University: New Foundations for Collegiality, Autonomy, and Achievement. Higher Education Management & Policy, 13(2), 9–24.

Clarysse, B., Wright, M. and Mustar, P. 2009. Behavioural additionality of R&D subsidies: A learning perspective. Research Policy, 38(10), 1517–1533.

Colyvas, J. A. 2007. From divergent meanings to common practices: The early institutionalization of technology transfer in the life sciences at Stanford University. Research Policy, 36(4), 456–476.

Davies, J. L. 2001. The Emergence of Entrepreneurial Cultures in European Universities. Higher Education Management, 13(2), 25–43.

Delanty, G. 2001. Challenging knowledge: the university in the knowledge society, Buckingham: Society for Research into Higher Education, Open University Press.

Doutriaux, J. 1987. Growth Pattern of Academic Entrepreneurial Firms. Journal of Business Venturing, 2(4), 285.

Drucker, P. F. 2007. Innovation and entrepreneurship: practice and principles, Rev. ed. Amsterdam ; London: Butterworth-Heinemann.

Druilhe, C. and Garnsey, E. 2004. Do Academic Spin-Outs Differ and Does It Matter? Journal of Technology Transfer, 29(3–4), 269–285.

Etzkowitz, H. 2003. Research groups as [`]quasi-firms': the invention of the entrepreneurial university. Research Policy, 32(1), 109–121.

Etzkowitz, H., Webster, A., Gebhardt, C. and Terra, B. R. C. 2000. The future of the university and the university of the future: evolution of ivory tower to entrepreneurial paradigm. Research Policy, 29(2), 313–330.

Fairweather, J. S. 1988. Entrepreneurship and higher education: lessons for colleges, universities, and industry: Association for the Study of Higher Education.

George, G., Jain, S. and Maltarich, M. 2005. Academics or Entrepreneurs? Entrepreneurial identity and invention disclosure behaviour of university scientists. Technology Transfer Society Conference. Kansas City.

Jain, S., George, G. and Maltarich, M. 2009. Academics or entrepreneurs? Investigating role identity modification of university scientists involved in commercialization activity. Research Policy, 38(6), 922–935.

Johnson, D. 2001a. What is innovation and entrpreneurship? Lessons for Larger Organisations. Industrial and Commercial Training, 33(4), 135–140.

Karlsson, T. and Wigren, C. 2010. Start-ups among university employees: the influence of legitimacy, human capital and social capital. The Journal of Technology Transfer, 1–16.

Koivula, J. and Rinne, R. 2006. Dilemmas of the Changing University. EUEREK (European Universities for Entrepreneurship: their role in the Europe of knowledge) [Online]. Available: http://www.euerek.info/Public_Documents/Documents/Changing%20university%201511%20.doc [Accessed 13/11/2010].

Martin, L. and Turner, P. 2010. Entrepreneurial universities the key ingredient in the recipe for UK innovation? Realities of working in business engagement roles in academia. The International Journal of Entrepreneurship and Innovation, 11(4), 273–281.

Rothaermel, F. T., Agung, S. D. and Jiang, L. 2007. University entrepreneurship: a taxonomy of the literature. Industrial & Corporate Change, 16(4), 691–791.

Schumpeter, J. 1950. Capitalism, Socialism, and Democracy, 3rd New York, NY: Harper and Row.

Shattock, M. 2009. Entrepreneurialism in universities and the knowledge economy: diversification and organizational change in European higher education, Maidenhead: Open University Press.

Shattock, M. 2010. Managing successful universities, 2nd ed. Maidenhead: Open University Press.

Siegel, D. S., Waldman, D. and Link, A. 2003. Assessing the impact of organizational practices on the relative productivity of university technology transfer offices: an exploratory study. Research Policy, 32(1), 27–48.

Siegel, D. S., Wright, M. and Lockett, A. 2007. The rise of entrepreneurial activity at universities: organizational and societal implications. Industrial & Corporate Change, 16(4), 489–504.

Warren, L., Kitagawa, F. and Eatough, M. 2010. Developing the knowledge economy through university linkages An exploration of RDA strategies through case studies of two English regions. The International Journal of Entrepreneurship and Innovation, 11(4), 293–306.

Whittle, A. and Mueller, F. 2008. Intra-preneurship and enrolment: building networks of ideas. Organization, 15(3), 445–462.

Wright, M., Clarysse, B., Mustar, P. and Lockett, A. 2007. Academic Entrepreneurship in Europe, Cheltenham, UK: Edward Elgar Publishing.

THE GOVERNANCE OF A GLOBALISED UNIVERSITY

Towards Global Localisation

Graham Baldwin and Rick Wylie

ABSTRACT

Many universities have a strategy for internationalisation, usually having begun with transnational education and overseas student recruitment. More recently, changes to higher education and related policies, a change in control by nation states and the increasing influence of globalisation has led to the development of strategies to include differing models such as overseas partnerships and the development of branch campuses. These models and the impact of globalisation, which bears upon all institutions, have required universities to consider and review their governance to ensure they can operate effectively beyond national boundaries and maintain their quality, reputation and brand whille meeting the needs of an increased range of stakeholders. This paper considers the impact of globalisation, its opportunities and implications and potential responses for the changing governance of increasingly international universities.

INTRODUCTION

Governance, it has been argued, has become one of the key issues in higher education, especially in the modern 'world class' university[1].

The expansion of student numbers, the diversification of provision, new modes of delivery such as e-learning, the heterogeneity of the student body, the increasing linkage with knowledge provision and technology transfer – all in addition to, and overlain by, the complexity of globalisation which bears upon universities at all levels – has meant that governance is a key factor in the success or otherwise of an institution as it confronts and positions itself in the new globalised marketplace.

Universities have a special relationship with the dynamics of globalisation. They are affected by the dynamics of the process as well as being its agents. Operating as nodes in global flows of easily portable and transmissible knowledge[2], universities can both fix and facilitate these movements, creating new configurations of knowledge development and dissemination beyond the scope and scale of institutions and across the boundaries of nations. They have potentially massive implications for the localities in which they are embedded, as well as the states which license their products and services.

This paper focuses upon the implications and opportunities of globalisation for the governance of universities, and considers the implications of globalisation for the governance of a contemporary university operating in multi-national settings.

GOVERNANCE

We use the term 'governance' in this paper to describe the process and structure created by the actors involved in governing a university. Today, the dynamics of globalisation, and the institutional imperative to respond to that dynamic, shapes the governance architecture beyond the boundaries of what might be considered a 'traditional' university with its essential 'triangle of co-ordination'[3] comprising system, institution and the academic community.

Today, within international and even globalising universities, organisational complexities have arisen. These are due to the reshaping and rescaling of the operations across international boundaries and the relationships the universities forge with licensing authorities in a number of nation states, while at the same time attempting to create and maintain the university's character, identity and unique selling point.

A governance perspective, which recognises the multiplicity and plurality of centres of power within governing networks, is about change, about responding to new problems and possibilities in the face of changes such as globalisation which rescales and reconfigures the operations creating new organisational and inter-organisational structures. We have moved beyond a view of the governance of a university simply as '...the process of decision making *within* an institution...'[4]. In contemporary society, the governance of a university needs to take account of wider influences which are *beyond* the traditional boundaries of a university, such as global markets for staff and students, which bear so heavily upon its operations at all levels.

Governance comprises the actions of the institution, plus its interaction with partners such as industry, private investors, local, regional and national governments and event organisations in the not-for-profit sector. This operational definition takes into account the wider context of globalised knowledge, markets and finance, and the multiple influences upon the institution and it broadens out the subject of this paper to include wider architectures of governance involving relationships with other organisations operating in an international environment within the context of the sometimes pernicious dynamics of globalisation.

Writing in 1998, Stoker presented five propositions to refer to systemic, national governance – all of which are relevant to this discussion of the governance of a globalised university. These five propositions give an insight into the character of governing and reveal a focus upon:

• a set of institutions and actors drawn from, but also beyond the institution;

- power dependence in the relationships between institutions;
- networks of actors;
- new tools and techniques to steer and guide, rather than command and authority;
- blurred boundaries and responsibilities.

University governance is, in some respects, a microcosm of issues confronting policymakers in regional, national and wider contexts, which involve multiple actors and sectors and comprise organisations with permeable boundaries and power dependencies. These dynamics create a potential lack of control by key actors and policy institutions and create imperatives for new, often market based, approaches to steer and govern universities. For example, in the United Kingdom new public management approaches such as the Research Excellence Framework and student loans increasingly influence management along with government policy which is increasing the marketisation of the sector.

THE GLOBALISED UNIVERSITY

Globalisation is essentially about communication and the flows of resources, information and images around the world[5]. It comprises actor networks of people, resources and technologies formed into hybrid 'assemblages' requiring new modes and models of governance, especially for the globalised university. Indeed, universities are globalised in many ways, from the markets for students, knowledge and research, to standards of excellence monitored by national organisations such as the UK QAA and ranked in league tables by the likes of the QS and THES. Indeed, as the market for university products and services stretches across the globe, and as universities compete and collaborate in globalised markets, they may be envisaged as global production networks.

At the same time, the global networks create systemic and structural pressures from new interactions and opportunities between individuals, places and institutions. These processes and pressures are at the heart of globalisation as a systemic phenomenon. In many respects, and in most regions, universities may be seen as both the objects of globalisation as well as its agents[6].

Through globalisation the relations between individuals and institutions are radically revised. This is especially the case within universities, with their role in the creation and dissemination of knowledge. The experience of space and time has already been stretched as social, economic and communication relations extend beyond a particular place, now radically demonstrated through the internet, through international movements of staff and students, and e-learning and perhaps most easily through the international flow of knowledge. The contemporary university is a key node in these glo-balised networks as they '(are) foundational to knowledge, (shape) the take up of technologies, (stimulate) cross-border association and... (consequently are key to) sustain complex communities'[7]. They have a vital relationship with their localities and nations as a consequence of this status as a clear correlation between presence and performance of regions[8]. In respect of culture, knowledge, tech-nology and citizenship, universities are key nodes on the 'scapes' of globalisation[9].

But is there such a thing as a global university? There are certainly parallels between the imperatives faced by an international uni-versity and those confronting a multi-national corporation (MNC) which, following Lao[10]:

- must deal with more demanding and more diverse global share-holders and stakeholders;
- have more complex governance structures that are subject to more institutional and strategic constraints;
- have multi-tier or multi-level governance systems, which jointly constitute their overall corporate governance framework;
- must establish and execute a larger number of governance mecha-nisms and instruments to cope with globalising needs and cross-country differences in governance norms;

• must configure corporate governance with a multitude of much more complicated strategies, structures and environments.

The key themes in the governance of an MNC, which resonate with the situation of a large comprehensive university, are the diversity, complexity and dispersion of shareholders and stakeholders. Adding to the complexity, and similar to an MNC, these are embedded in a range of national settings, each with different norms, regulations and cultures and these are configured into often unique assemblages of actors requiring a complex governance architecture.

GLOBALISING OR WORLD CLASS?

One element in the discussion of a global university is the concept of 'world class'. This can be defined or measured in a variety of ways, though measures at the moment are not agreed or formal; they tend to be prepared by the media and used as a marketing tool. It is clear that universities do not largely dissent with regard to the scales, particularly those which are at the top of the tables and, as Deem et al noted, 'Everyone wants a world-class university... the problem is that no one knows what (one) is..."[11]. The notion of a world class university seems elusive. As David Watson, former vice-chancellor of the University of Brighton in the UK, suggested, "world-class" [he said] is one of those things which apparently, you know... when you see ..."[12].

Actually, given the importance of research in the identification of a world class university, and the quality of student experience alongside it, rankings like QS rate universities on a uniform scale in respect of what one would suppose a university ought to be. Thus, the higher placed are not necessarily physically larger or have a presence overseas, and may operate internationally mainly through research. In reality they may have fewer overseas students (particularly undergraduates) in total than many of the 'modern' universities at the lower end of the tables. Universities like Oxbridge and MIT

tend to be the highest in scales like QS and the THES as a consequence of their reputations established through research. Thus, these
global scales and rankings give only one indication of a global university experience. That said, these rankings can be very important
to a university.

Watson[13] cited a document published by the UK government in
2004, 'Putting the World into World Class Education'. In this document it was proposed that three main things are involved in a world
class education:

- understanding the world in which we live: the values and cultures
  of different societies and the ways in which we all, as global citizens, can influence and shape the changes in the global economy,
  environment and society of which we are part;
- knowing what constitutes world-class educational standards, mea-
  suring ourselves against them and matching them; and
- being a global partner overseas[14].

The development of an internationalised university ranges from
insitu internationalisation through the acquisition of students from
abroad onto a home campus – or to study online from a foreign
university[15]. Perhaps one of the key differences here is between globalisation and internationalisation.

Following Marginson and van der Vende[16], the term 'international' refers to any relationship across borders between nations,
or between single institutions situated within different national systems. This contrasts with globalisation, the processes of world-wide
engagement and convergence associated with the growing role of
global systems that criss-cross many national borders. Internationalisation can involve as few as two units, whereas globalisation takes
in many nations and is a dynamic process drawing the local, national
and global dimensions more closely together[17].

Globalisation is more obviously transformative than internationalisation, which is both less transformative and less culturally loaded
than globalisation. The former implies a cross-border relationship

between institutions situated within national systems – within the model of a world of nation states, which maintain university functions as independent cultural, political and economic systems. It does not remake, remap or rescale relationships or organisations as globalisation does, where borders are permeable and power relationships fluid. Moreover, one is more in control of the internationalisation agenda which, in a university context, means heterogeneity of experience, and a multicultural agenda in addition to access to global networks of educational resources.

Globalisation is, in contrast, a more pervasive process which transcends nation states. It is, crucially, uncontrollable while internationalisation is (in a university context) within the grasp, grip and gift of the management of a university. In a globalised world, dynamic processes of change[18] create significant pressures on the governance of an organisation as new relationships, processes and players bear upon the university.

In the global higher education arena the international agenda suggests a relationship between extant organisations that connect through cross-border mobility of students and scholars and may be without the integrative thrust of globalisation. This interpretation is consistent with Scott[19] who argues that internationalisation refers to processes of greater cooperation between states and activities which take place across borders[20]. Globalisation, on the other hand, refers primarily to the processes of increasing interdependence, and ultimately convergence of economies and to the liberalisation of trade and markets[21]. It is this convergence which is a paradox of globalisation and which drives to the heart of governance in a globalised environment.

It may also be that globalisation goes beyond the development of national programmes and their sale to international students, or offering experiences in other (national) universities – or indeed of offering national programmes in different localities. It may be that the globalisation agenda provides opportunities for developing a globalised appreciation and sensibility, and preparing learners and students for an interconnected and interdependent world[22], preparing individuals (staff and students) for citizenship in a globalised world – far more than just the development of an international student experience.

Indeed, the modern international university has, it is argued[23] an opportunity to develop a globalised sense of citizenship, a crucially important, if rather nebulous, concept. That said, a global sensibility and orientation is prized by employers. A 2011 survey for the British Council revealed that a global sensibility and awareness is at least as important as degree classification or A-levels[24].

THE GOVERNANCE OF A GLOBAL UNIVERSITY

Earlier, we conceptualised a university at a nexus between the global, the national and the local. A governance perspective foregrounds the importance and role of the networks involving those levels, and focuses upon the spaces between organisations and stakeholders.

We have also already mentioned the new public management techniques of marketisation and performance used as a form of controlling the wider governance of the HE sector as authorities employ steering at the macro level through, among other things, controls on student numbers and nationally imposed legislation limiting the scope and scale of the university such as fees arrangements. These activities have potentially reduced the autonomy of scholars and, over recent years, there has been a shift in the governance of universities away from the concept of a community of scholars to become supplanted by a cadre of professional managers and external stakeholders.

Additionally, despite the globalisation and internationalisation of HE, the role of the nation state is still central to the sector and to universities through their licensing and award of title and status to higher education institutions. Such control by these central authorities can create, through measures such as student control numbers and national fee regimes, an imperative for the entrepreneurial university to look overseas for expansion. Indeed, the marketisation and internationalisation of HE in general at a time of declining state support for universities in many countries and a greater competition among universities, and in the sector in general, is potentially creating a pressure for universities to expand internationally[25].

Thus, the internationalisation agenda has created significant implications in respect of the governance of a university, as it responds to this new agenda by rescaling its activities through new developments such as franchises, joint ventures and expansion through foreign direct investment. Today, drawing upon Clark's classic study of university organisation[26], which stressed the 'triangle' of coordination – 'market-like' coordination, i.e. a response to demand from students and families; state-induced coordination; and academic professional coordination – the influence of the professoriate and the professional administration of universities. Clearly, with the move towards a more entrepreneurial university, and a decline in the influence of the professoriate and community of scholars in the governance of the university, a fourth element – external stakeholders – has emerged as crucially important. This category would include, inter alia, communities, industry, professional bodies and the media. This opens out the governance of the university to a much wider community.

Today, external stakeholders play an increasingly central role in the governance of universities, often as board members[27] and we can see these influences in different modes of university governance. Following Trakmman[28] there are a number of classic modes of university governance:

- Faculty – the most traditional form of governance, principally by academic staff;
- Corporate – focus on fiscal and managerial responsibility and efficiency – a business case model involving a CEO and SMT;
- Trustee – refers to the manner of governance with individual trustees having a fiduciary duty to manage with a focus on confidence and trust; and

- Stakeholder – governance vested in a wide array of stakeholders, staff, students, alumni, corporate partners, public, government.

In the UK, we see elements of all of these modes of university governance, but increasingly subsumed into more complex, hybrid structures.

BRITISH UNIVERSITY GOVERNANCE

There are a number of different governance arrangements among British universities, reflecting a difference in the legal status and constitution of different types of university. The older, 'pre-1992' universities were established by Royal Charter, the 'post-92' universities were formed as Higher Education Corporations (HECs) by virtue of an act of parliament and some of the most recently formed universities have been established as companies limited by guarantee.

The pre-92s, established by Royal Charter, usually have a governance structure that includes the university court, the university council and the senate. Essentially, the council is the equivalent of a board and is the decision-making body with regard to the financial and business-related aspects. It also has responsibility for the overall shape and nature of the institution. Approximately two members of the court would be members of council. The court meets once a year and brings together 'the great and the good' of the region, key local stakeholders from government, the community and industry to hear about the university's performance and to question its activities. A council is chaired by the pro-chancellor (the chancellor is a figurehead) and the senate is responsible for academic aspects of the university and is chaired by the vice-chancellor. The senate leads on the academic character and nature of the university and is made up of representatives from within the university with the vice-chancellor acting as the link between the senate and council.

Post-92 HECs are similar but few have a formal court. They tend to have a university board which is equivalent to council. These also have an independent chair (again, a pro-chancellor) and are made up of a number of people from differing walks of life but usually would include individuals with an expertise in finance, legal and HR matters as well as general management. The academic aspects of the university are managed through the academic board, chaired by the vice-chancellor who is the link between the board and the academic board. Again, there is a figurehead chancellor.

Most boards have a number of committees, the most common and important being audit or audit and risk committee. Other common committees include resources, and all the boards have a search and remuneration committee. Some universities have been moving towards a more streamlined approach and adopting the Carver or adapted Carver structure which has fewer committees and more frequent meetings of a smaller board. The university board consists of university employees as well as the vice-chancellor. Other members of the executive can attend for part or all of meetings depending on the agenda.

Reflecting the diversity of activities of a university, and of particular interest in this discussion of the rescaling of a university there may an increasing number of external bodies. Institutions may, for example, have a number of subsidiary companies which have been created largely to either provide security for the university and the HEC by keeping some business ventures at arm's length or as tax efficiency vehicles.

Companies can be joint ventures with different investment models both to comply with local legal requirements and because the aims can be subtly different. They would normally have their own board and shareholder agreement. The university would always have control of the academic activity and can be paid an academic service fee by the company. The partner directors have input into the non-academic business developments. A significant risk with such overseas activity is in the quality and, therefore, reputation of the host university, which is why complete control of the academic quality assurance procedures is essential. Thus, in partnership arrangements, the role of the scholars and academic systems is key to the success of the international venture. It underscores the importance of the wider academic community in ensuring the successful governance and management, as well as operation, of an academic business whether it be at home or overseas.

GLOBALISATION AND LOCALISATION

We have argued that the marketisation of the HE sector, and policy pressures at home have led many universities to seek to expand abroad. This marketisation is reflected in the actors involved in the governance structure of the university, the increasing focus on employability and the conception of students as customers for services. These developments have created new pressures on universities domestically as a range of stakeholders are involved in the governance process: they have also created an imperative to expand overseas with consequent complexity in the governance structures of the institution.

One of the key issues is the portability of the USP and the relationship between the USP and a globalising student experience beyond that of the national or international. There may be, however, a fundamental issue for a globalising university – the maintenance of the character and values of the institution, delivered and experienced in a range of localities in foreign settings. This rescaling of the activities of a university requires a new approach to the governance of the institution which will need to incorporate international partners, collaborators and stakeholders in the governance architecture of the institution.

A globalising university becomes a hybrid, driven and shaped as much by the activities abroad as by those at home. This hybrid nature of the international activities may come to shape the governance of the university through the international activities shaping the policy of the home institution. There is the prospect of a truly globalising university structure. Earlier, we drew upon Stoker's[29] five propositions of governance which we extended to a university context:

- a set of institutions and actors drawn from but also beyond the institution;
- power dependence in the relationships between institutions;
- networks of actors;
- new tools and techniques to steer and guide, rather than command and authority;
- blurred boundaries and responsibilities.

We argued that a key element of these propositions is that the organisation is involved in wider processes and new types of relationship with a plurality and diversity of actors, with which it had a dependent relationship, in order to achieve its goals. Clearly, this is especially relevant to a flexible, globalising university operating a range of multinational settings, especially an institution less concerned with the portability of its (possibly place-bound) unique selling proposition.

In such an institution, the governance architecture must embrace a wide range of actors in both the non-host country campuses as well as the host country campus itself as it comes to offer a globalising student experience. The institution becomes a network of organisations, actors and individuals whose responsibilities and organisational positions become increasingly blurred.

This begins to offer the prospect of a globalising university operating in localities around the world, whose governance architecture comes to create a key element in the potential for a globalising student experience, an experience highly prized by employers operating in a globalised commercial environment. Academic staff, for example, will increasingly operate in a rescaled context, disembedded from their national settings, as global workers[30] and that experience will form part of the academic product of the university.

CONCLUSION

Today, modern universities sit at a nexus between the pull of globalisation, the push of regionalism and, in the UK, the pressures of national educational policy change. This complex dynamic creates an imperative for the rescaling and reconstituting of governance architectures of globalised and globalising institutions.

Globalisation may, it is argued, lead towards a uniformity of experience and the 'McDonaldisation' and homogenisation of experience through the operation of global markets. In a discussion of universities globally, this is exemplified by the QS and THES global university ratings, which provide a common benchmark of educational standards across the globe. This is a narrower perspective to that of a world class education which embraces an understanding of the world and the values and cultures of various societies and individuals as global citizens being empowered to shape the global economy, environment and society. 'World class' is also a statement of the perceived quality of the work undertaken but in many cases it is difficult to define, difficult to determine and difficult to identify. Institutions can be undeniably internationalising within a global context but may not be perceived as world class by virtue of the narrow definitions assigned or because, as already stated, it is difficult to identify. The very process of internationalisation by developing beyond national boundaries and the offering of similar experiences elsewhere may indeed militate against a perception of world class, particularly where excellence is synonymous with specific individuals or place. Internationalisation by universities embraces the notion of global partnerships. This global-localisation concept has significant implications for the governance architecture of a university which could be a centripetal dynamic which draws together the international elements of a geographically dispersed university. Such structures need to embrace localities and regions while also operating in a globalised world system. The challenge in any institution adopting such models will be maintaining appropriate balance and oversight of the overall group operation and balancing the differing strengths of each component and the potentially differing perceptions of the importance and quality of each. However, such a *globalising* university would have the potential to create a genuinely globalising student experience prized by employers which is embedded in regions and places around the world and provide the opportunity for enhanced reputation, greater control and long-term sustainability for the players involved.

NOTES

1. Marginson and van der Wende, 2007.
2. Urry, 2010.
3. Sporn, 2010.
4. Trakman, 2008, emphasis added.
5. Urry, 2010.
6. Marginson, 2010.
7. Marginson, 2010.
8. Marginson, 2010.
9. Urry, 2010.
10. Lao, 2006.
11. Deem et al, 2008, page 21.
12. Watson, 2006.
13. Watson, 2006.
14. Cited in Deem et al, 2008.
15. OECD Observer Policy Brief, 2004.
16. Vende, 2007.
17. Marginson and Rhoades, 2002.
18. Duit and Galaz, 2008.
19. Scott, 1998.
20. Enders, 2004.
21. Enders, 2004.
22. Trahar and Hyland, 2011.
23. Trahar and Hyland, 2011.
24. Think Global and the British Council, 2011.
25. Bleiklie and Kogan, 2007.

26. Clark, 1983.
27. Sporn, 2010.
28. Trakmman, 2008.
29. Stoker, 1998.
30. Jones, 2008.

REFERENCES

Bleikliea, I. and Kogan, M. (2007) 'Organization and Governance of Universities', *Higher Education Policy*, 20: 477–493.

Buckley, P. J. and Strange, R. (2011) 'The Governance of the Multinational Enterprise: Insights from Internalization Theory'' *Journal of Management Studies* 48(2): 460–470.

Carnegie, Garry D. and Tuck, J. (2010) 'Understanding the ABC of University Governance', *The Australian Journal of Public Administration*, vol. 69,(4): 431–441.

Chiang, L. (2012) 'Trading on the West's Strength: The Dilemmas of Transnational Higher Education in East Asia', *Higher Education Policy*, 25: 171–189.

Clark, B.R. (1983). The Higher Education System: *Academic Organization in Cross-National Perspective*. Berkeley, California: University of California Press.

Deem, R., Mok, K. H. and Lucas, L. (2008) 'Transforming Higher Education in Whose Image? Exploring the Concept of the 'World-Class' University in Europe and Asia', *Higher Education Policy*, 21: 83–97.

Duit, A. and Galaz, V. (2008) 'Governance and complexity: Emerging issues for governance theory', Governance: An International *Journal of Policy, Administration, and Institutions* 21(3):311–335.

Enders, J. (2004) 'Higher education, internationalisation, and the nation-state: Recent developments and challenges to governance theory'. *Higher Education* 47: 361–382.

Fazekas, M. and Burns, T. (2012), "Exploring the Complex Interaction Between Governance and Knowledge in Education", *OECD Education Working Papers*, No. 67, OECD Publishing. http://dx.doi.org/10.1787/5k9flcx2l340–en.

Hénard, F. and Mitterle, A. (2010) Governance And Quality Guidelines In Higher Education A Review Of Governance Arrangements And Quality Assurance Guidelines www.oecd.org/edu/imhe/46064461.pdf.

Jones, A. (2008) The rise of global work. *Transactions of the Institute of British Geographers* 33: 12–26.

Jones, G. A. (2008) Can Provincial Universities be Global Institutions? Rethinking the Institution as the Unit of Analysis in the Study of Globalization and Higher Education. *Higher Education Policy*, 21: 457–468.

Kumar, S. and Seth, A. (1998) The Design Of Coordination And Control Mechanisms For Managing Joint Venture–Parent Relationships. *Strategic Management Journal* 19: 579–599.

Kiel, G. C. Hendry, K. and Nicholson, G. J. (2006) Corporate governance options for the local subsidiaries of multinational enterprises. *Corporate Governance: An International Review* 14 (6): 568–576.

King, R. (2011) Power and Networks in Worldwide Knowledge Coordination: The Case of Global Science. *Higher Education Policy* 24: 359–376.

Lao, Y. (2005) Corporate governance and accountability in multinational enterprises: Concepts and agenda. *Journal of International Management* 1: 1–18.

Marginson, S. and Rhoades, G. (2002) Beyond national states, markets, and systems of higher education: A glonacal agency heuristic. *Higher Education* 43: 281–309.

Marginson, S. (2006) Dynamics of national and global competition in higher education. *Higher Education* 52: 1–39.

Marginson, S. and van der Wende M. (2007) "Globalisation and Higher Education", *OECD Education Working Papers*, No. 8, OECD Publishing. http://dx.doi.org/10.1787/173831738240.

Mohrman, K., Wanhua, M and Baker, D (2008) The Research University in Transition: The Emerging Global Model. *Higher Education Policy* 21: 5–27.

Mok, K. H. (2012) The Rise of Transnational Higher Education in Asia: Student Mobility and Studying Experiences in Singapore and Malaysia. *Higher Education Policy* 25: 225–241.

OECD Policy Brief (2004) Internationalisation of Higher Education. http://www.oecd.org/education/country-studies/33734276.pdf.

Onga, K. C. and Chan, D.K. (2012) Transnational Higher Education and Challenges for University Governance in China. *Higher Education Policy* 25: 151–170.

Salmi, J. (2009) The Challenge of Establishing World-Class Universities. Washington D.C.: The International Bank for Reconstruction and Development and The World Bank.

Scott, P. (2000) Globalisation and Higher Education: Challenges for the 21st Century. *Journal of Studies in International Education* 4(1): 3–10.

Stoker, G. (1998) Governance as Theory: Five propositions. *International Social Science Journal* 50(155): 17–28.

Swyngedouw, E. (2004) Globalisation or 'Glocalisation'? Networks, Territories and Rescaling. *Cambridge Review of International Affairs* 17 (1): 25–48.

Think Global and British Council (2011) The Global Skills Gap Preparing young people for the new global economy. Accessed at http://www.think-global.org.uk/resources/item.asp?d=6404.

Trahar, S. and Hyland, F. (2011) 'Experiences and Perceptions of Internationalisation in Higher Education in the UK'. *Higher Education Research and Development*, 30: 623–633.

Trakman, L. (2008) Modelling University Governance. *Higher Education Quarterly* 62, (1/2): 63–83.

Urry, J. (2010) Mobile Sociology. *The British Journal of Sociology* 61 (S1): 347–366.

Van Vught, F. (2008) Mission Diversity and Reputation in Higher Education. *Higher Education Policy* 21: 151–174.

Watson, D. (2006) 'UK higher education: the truth about the student market', *Higher Education Review* 38(3): 3–16.

Westnesa, P., Hatakenakab, S., Gjelsvika, M. and Lester, R K. (2009) The Role of Universities in Strengthening Local Capabilities for Innovation – A Comparative Case Study. H*igher Education Policy* 22: 483–503.

UNIVERSITIES IMPACTING ON THEIR REGION – A CASE STUDY

The North West Universities Association (1999 to 2012)

David Briggs and Keith Burnley

The North West Universities Association (NWUA) operated from early 1999 to March 2012. It was established in response to the development of the regional agenda in England and its operations largely followed the objectives of the 1997–2010 government's regional economic growth strategies.

From the time of the 1997 election it had been clear that significant resources and political control were to be vested in new structures and functions targeted on stimulating sustainable growth in and through the regions. In response by early 2000 most of the nine English regions saw Higher Education Regional Associations set up to strengthen the voice of universities and to provide a vehicle for engagement with newly emerging regional stakeholders and partners.

Underlying government and consequent regional policy was a belief that economic development and the welfare of regions could and should be enhanced through universities' various engagement with the regional and local economy. This included research, infrastructure development, education, effective industry partnerships, technological innovation and community engagement. However, these arose with little understanding of existing processes, the context or complexities of actors or how regional economic development could actually be achieved through better utilisation of university expertise.

Eighteen years on, it is sometimes difficult to appreciate the relatively limited view held of universities in the late 1990s as contributors to economic growth and as crucial actors in innovation. Nor is it well remembered that policy authors had only limited understanding of the actual processes of knowledge flows and raised few questions over the detail of how economic development could benefit and be achieved through better exploitation of university knowledge. The view of universities held by many senior civil servants, council officers, politicians and business people harked back to their own experience in the 1960s and early 1970s. While there was an acceptance of the strategic imperative for universities to engage, in practice many universities were at an embryonic stage in relation to the development of the necessary processes and support mechanisms.

Concepts such as the triple helix of civic, business and university impact and 'third stream' were only just emerging at both national and regional levels. They only became a strong policy aspiration as universities established a central role as partners in the drive for economic and social development.

It is this space that NWUA sought to occupy, and in the north west the scale and range of higher education, the vigour with which wider stakeholders took to the agenda and the availability of significant European structural funds arguably brought about one of the most robust, successful and high impact HE Regional Associations in the country.

From the outset, the NWUA board determined that association activity was to add value over and above what could be achieved by institutions acting independently. This principle remained unchanged throughout operations and provided the organisation with the freedom and authority to develop, facilitate and effect new joint activities and collaborations.

In this chapter we discuss firstly the general impact that NWUA had on the north-west region, secondly how it influenced national policy and finally details of some of its major projects.

The sustained impact of NWUAs activity in the region was achieved through the successful and effective long term relationships that it established at strategic and operational level with a wide range of key partners and stakeholders. As well as working closely with key agencies of local and national government, in particular the North West Regional Development Agency (NWDA), the North West Regional Assembly, and Government Office for the North West (GONW), relationships were established with a wide range of regional organisations representing business and civil society.

Key to this process was the establishment at various stages of strategy and policy groups[1], bringing together expertise and experience that would not have been available at individual institution level, to consider the wide-ranging agendas emerging from English regionalism. These groups, whose membership at any one time exceeded 150 individuals, provided a bridge between strategic, tactical and operational agendas. They developed as melting pots for ideas and approaches and much was learnt between institutions that in early stages seemed less than 'natural partners'. The groups were closely involved in NWUA-led projects, examples of which are given below, at both the development and operational stage.

The association succeeded in demonstrating to NWDA that the higher education sector could adapt to circumstances and articulate a collective breadth of view that was far beyond that assumed in the early stages. This allowed negotiation of valuable contracts and partnerships with a level of flexibility that provided great benefit to both organisations and their stakeholders. NWUA earned a reputation as an organisation with the ability to organise and deliver beyond its more obvious brief and that could be trusted as a source of confidential intelligence.

NWUA was the natural vehicle by which university interests were represented in regional fora and was a member of the North West Regional Assembly. This widespread engagement contributed significantly to the association's long-term ability to build high-impact coalitions with a wide range of partner organisations and stakeholders.

Following the demonstration of successful regional engagement, the key staff and senior representatives of the membership became increasingly engaged with Westminster and Whitehall as a source of informed and sophisticated advice and guidance while building perceptions of the north-west association as an organisation valued both to run projects and represent the interests of the membership.

The board of NWUA empowered the association to operate at the highest possible level of influence which enabled it to make connections into parliament, Whitehall and high-level business environments that were often not accessed by other Regional Higher Education Associations. NWUA regularly engaged with HEFCE and Universities UK by providing formal and informal responses to requests for information, consultation and intelligence. Over the years HEFCE and other national bodies regularly took advantage of the existence of the wide-ranging network of NWUA strategy and policy groups. Many senior HEFCE staff were welcome and regular attendees at NWUA meetings and used the structure at board and group level as a test bed for many national issues.

Thus NWUA provided a valuable resource for the Funding Council by accurately and efficiently canvassing its membership, gleaning their perspectives and speaking with one voice. The impact of the association's relationship enabled it to often be a first 'port of call' for commentary and to negotiate above its weight for national project contracts to benefit north-west universities and the region as a whole. It also enabled it to be one of the better-heard voices in some of the dialogue about the future direction of higher education in the United Kingdom.

There was also direct engagement with government and parliament. A programme of highly successful parliamentary events was organised by the association hosted by members of parliament (MPs) from all parties. This in turn led to a programme of briefings for MPs targeted on regional elected members to keep them up to date and aware of the issues and progress of the sector in the north-west and as an important part of the national university network.

Turning to the final and main subject of this chapter, NWUA projects, presents the authors with the unenviable task of selecting, for reasons of brevity, a small number of projects from a large and diverse portfolio of activities that impacted upon the region. We have chosen six projects that, hopefully, give a flavour of the range and diversity of the activities: Knowledge North West, the Higher Level Skills Partnership, the HE/Business Engagement Project, the Leonardo da Vinci mobility programme, the Economic Downturn Project and European Structural Fund engagement.

The first major success of NWUA was the approval of a bid to HEFCE for the establishment of a Knowledge and Skills Brokerage Service, which then evolved with NWDA funding into Knowledge North West. These projects developed a route to quick and complete connections for business and others into the higher education sector expertise, handling in excess of 2,700 enquiries during their lifetime.

Through its marketing and promotion activity across the north-west, the service also contributed to accelerating the level of awareness of HEI capabilities and their specific services amongst intermediaries and representative bodies, demonstrating the breadth of collective expertise and giving profile to higher education through the association.

KNW processes and staff demonstrated excellent customer care of SMEs and others and guided them through a complex and potentially difficult environment as local university systems were developed. As these matured, universities built their own portfolios of client companies and institutions and, as these tailored and bespoke offers became clearer, the need for a single regional access point diminished.

The experience was valuable in the process of negotiation and development of several later successes, most notably the Higher Level Skills Partnership (HLSP) and access to the European Regional Development Funds, each of which had characteristics that related to KNW services but were improved and informed by the KNW experience.

NWUA, perhaps, achieved its highest point of influence and engagement when it participated as a high-impact player, not only at regional but at national level, in the HLSP initiative.

The north-west HLSP was one of three regional pathfinder projects funded for three years by HEFCE from 2006. The NWUA-led project successfully linked higher education into the established regional skills infrastructures and increased access to education and training provision to meet identified workforce development needs. The initial success of the initiative enabled NWUA to win further funding from NWDA that enhanced and extended HLSP activities through to March 2011.

The project brought together NWUA members with a large range of regional partners, including the Association of Colleges, the North West (Skills) Provider Network, Sector Skills Councils, GONW, the NWDA, Business Link NW, Learning and Skills Councils and the Regional Skills and Employment Board.

The HLSP was truly demand-led: its core innovative feature was development and delivery based on seeking expressions of interest from providers (not just the NWUA membership) to develop courses against a published 'prospectus' agreed with employers. The adoption of an assessment panel process involving appropriate partners, but not the universities themselves, was unique. It was also potentially 'courageous', especially when of the first 40 applications submitted by member universities only nine were approved.

The association tackled the potentially difficult situation by then facilitating a rigorous second round process and by helping with data and supporting information and intelligence including labour market information. The process stimulated the spread of pockets of good practice within and between institutions and enabled cross fertilisation of approaches.

The early disappointments for some HEIs and the subsequent support from the association truly focused a number of HEI minds at both senior and operational level on how to work better to identify real employer need. The support processes also stimulated new levels of business engagement not only in course design and development processes but in delivery as well.

The experience was a reality check for many university teams and had long-term positive effects on their future approaches to working with sectors, relationships with employers and sector representatives. New connections were made between several academic teams and employers as a direct result of the NWUA approach to the initiative, many of which resulted in further take-up of future courses and other business services.

The success of the initiative was formally recognised in several ways including Balfour Beatty winning the NW Construction Award for Skills and Education for their interaction with the programme. NW HLSP projects featured in the key 2009 CBI document – Stepping Higher – and culminated with NWUA winning the Times Higher Award for Outstanding Employer Engagement on behalf of the membership in 2010.

These achievements were the pinnacle of the development of 70 new demand-led courses involving 11 universities, 13 FE colleges and seven private training providers. Over 450 employers were actively engaged and invested the equivalent of over £1.5 million in cash and kind that resulted in over 4,000 employees receiving training. HLSP funding paid for development and design work, academic time, professional body accreditation and marketing.

The qualitative achievement of HLSP lay in facilitating new levels of close and collaborative working between companies and HEIs using public funding support. The volumes and levels of interest generated evidence of real employer support and engagement that made a tangible difference for employers and employees alike across the whole of the north-west region.

Over its extended life of nearly six years, the HLSP initiative not only met and exceeded all of its contracted targets but it positively altered many organisational perspectives both within universities and among employers that had little history of working with higher education. Equally importantly, a very substantial number of individuals both in work and seeking work were in receipt of valuable, highly relevant work-focused learning that enhanced their career opportunities and personal economic impact.

The HEFCE-and-NWDA-funded HE Business Engagement project, which operated alongside the HLSP between 2006 and 2009, was designed to support cluster engagement by higher education across seven industrial sectors.

By working with Business Link, recruiting academic advisers and engaging with sector bodies, the project succeeded in building new levels of connection between HEIs and professional services, digital and creative industries, environmental technology, sport, food and drink, advanced engineering and tourism companies.

One key aspect of this project, which built on an early innovation by NWUA, was the design and production of sector-focused HEI capability matrices, often published in brochure format. These were an effective and efficient response to the loudly voiced external demand for easily accessible 'first contact' information on the range of sectoral support services available to businesses from all HEIs in the region.

The concept was challenging given the breadth, volume and diversity of north-west HEIs offers and required a series of matrices to be developed that comprehensively showcased the resource. The approach taken was to arrange and sort the huge amount of information available according to the interests and demand of the sectors themselves, as opposed to the supply-side drivers of universities. This was achieved through close liaison with sector representation bodies and their membership and negotiation with each relevant HEI department to place their particular expertise in the 'right place'.

At times this was not just a logistical exercise but one requiring high levels of diplomacy as individual HEIs and departments jockeyed for position and profile in the final publication. However, the skills and integrity of NWUA staff ensured that all interests were addressed and the resulting documents were universally welcomed.

For external intermediary audiences, such as Business Link, the capability brochures proved to be a popular and very effective mechanism for HEI services and support to sectors to be promoted. They were catalysts for relationship building and some sector representative bodies, for example the north-west Aerospace Alliance and Chemicals north-west, regularly requested updates as they added so much value to their organisations service to members.

By representing the full range of north-west HEI expertise, the process also enabled the higher education sector never to leave a 'blank line' in any matrix and all of industries' articulated needs were met to some degree by the collective presentation of north-west universities capacity.

The project also developed networks of academics to support cluster organisations and regional agencies in relation to knowledge transfer and skills, and brought together universities and businesses in a series of events for example, a series of creative industries breakfast events held across the region.

In achieving all its objectives, and providing learning and opportunity for both the university sector and regional partners, the business engagement project was a valuable example of how the association sought out resources, built a partnership-based delivery structure and won positive outcomes for companies in target sectors which gave profile and impact for the collective of universities.

We now turn to an example of where a European programme without any explicit regional dimension was moulded to support the regional agenda. In 2003 NWUA took over responsibility for the Greater Manchester Leonardo da Vinci mobility programme, which developed and supported staff exchanges between UK and European universities designed to help develop competencies or innovative methods in vocational training. The programme also funded student work placements through programmes for students and recent graduates.

Subsequently, a new, NWUA-led regional Leonardo programme was approved for student and staff placements directly linked to regional economic strategy priority sectors. Additionally, links were made to increase the complementarities between the programme and wider NWUA agendas.

Outcomes included student placements to 11 countries in 2004 and a further set of student placements to 14 countries and staff exchanges to 19 countries in 2005. Over 1,000 individuals were involved in placements between December 1996 and May 2008.

The economic downturn of the mid to late 2000s brought a new opportunity for a regional response. In 2008 HEFCE sought to establish 'barometer' work through all Higher Education Regional Associations (HERAs), whereby the activity of universities in relation to mitigating the impact of the economic downturn could be recorded and reported to government on a quarterly basis. This approach included further opportunity for HERAs to make proposals for additional funding that would have a positive impact on the agenda in their regions.

In response, NWUA developed the concept of the Economic Downturn Project which included a proposal to leverage existing HLSP resources by ring-fencing £400,000 of its funding for the Redundancy Response Fund which then took a non-sectoral focus on re-skilling and up-skilling opportunities for those facing redundancy or who were at risk of losing their jobs. A steering group made up of unions, Job Centre Plus, careers services and others was established, building on the foundations of long-term good relations made over the years between the association and these key regional stakeholders.

Building on past experience and expertise, the pre-existing HLSP assessment process was adopted. This enabled a quicker response for both funders and applicants and the rapid development of new opportunities for the individual participants. Examples included re-skilling for aerospace and automotive technicians to move into the nuclear industry in Lancashire, and the development of digital printing expertise in the Greater Manchester area. Overall, contracts for work-based training to more than 500 learners were established and delivered.

The overall Economic Downturn Project also enabled the facilitation of dialogue with regional partners, resulting in the leverage of other additional regional resource, including a £3.5 million ESF Graduate Employability Support Programme.

Perhaps the most lasting impact of NWUA was in relation to European structural funding. NWUA was able to identify and advise both members and wider regional stakeholders when European funding was the right solution and when it was not, where flexibility existed and where ill-defined objectives could lead to difficulties. As a result, NWUA became an acknowledged regional expert on an 'unforgiving' funding scheme.

This ability required well-honed translation skills. Academic language could be difficult to understand for large funding bodies, while in turn the idiosyncrasies of European funding language could be open to misinterpretation by university staff. To articulate the complex and intricate aspects of HE operations and priorities and their multi-integrated nature to relatively young and newly established regional organisations was an outstanding skill.

The early insight and sharing of intelligence that were the hallmark of the NWUA service to its members gave HEIs more thinking time to develop project concepts. It enabled NWUA to lead and advise on new bidding opportunities, some of which had very short timescales.

NWUA successfully walked the narrow path of providing advice and support in a potentially competitive environment between HEIs. The association ensured that all members had equal information on opportunities, processes, systems and intelligence and yet gave local support to maximise the likelihood of success of particular projects.

NWUA brought substantial economies of scale for the university membership in helping them deliver successful projects without breaching rules and criteria and providing highly cost-effective support to administration processes.

While the association was engaged across the objective 1, 2 and 3 programmes, its major influence was felt in relation to the Objective 2 Knowledge Based Action Plan and later the Regional Action Plan.

The Knowledge Based Action Plan was formally transferred to NWUA from the Greater Manchester university-based CONTACT Partnership in 2003. With this came responsibility for the oversight of 53 revenue projects, 10 capital projects and the staff responsible for the support and dissemination of guidance on systems, audit trails and accountability. By the end of 2004 as the KBAP role shifted to more monitoring and scrutiny, the association could report accurately and confidently on behalf of its membership results of 2,930 new jobs and 3,655 safeguarded, SME sales of £253 million, a further £182 million safeguarded and a significant increase in the role of HE in supporting business.

In 2004 GONW initiated discussion on delivery of the second phase of the north-west Objective 2 programme for 2005–8. GONW and NWDA were agreed that it was necessary to seek a better and more co-ordinated regional approach to administration and delivery. This was to include a process of commissioning projects against a regional gaps and needs analysis.

In response, based on the strength of their preceding relationship, NWUA and NWDA agreed to establish a partnership for delivery under a single Regional Action Plan. It was agreed that NWUA would administer the distribution and management of allocations to Measure 1.4 (£23m) and Measure 3.1. (£8m) and these arrangements were finally approved in late December 2004.

The process of fund allocation was completed through four bidding rounds. Frameworks were established for sever sector/cluster areas, stimulating a range of new links between HEIs, sector support agencies and wider regional stakeholders and achieving a higher level of strategically coordinated regional delivery in the commissioning of business support, increased knowledge transfer and innovation and the engagement of SMEs.

By the close of the programme, NWUA and its membership were able to celebrate major success, achievement in the delivery of all Measure 1.4 targets amounting to 4,700 SMEs assisted; 2,017 new products/processes introduced; 5,867 jobs safeguarded; £430 million of sales safeguarded. Meanwhile, for Measure 3.1 the higher education sector achieved 99 per cent spend and 144 per cent of the required jobs created target to balance only 80 per cent of the jobs safeguarded against target.

Following the change in national government in 2010, the association continued to support its members as the regional agenda diminished and the new driving forces of government policy, city-regionalism and Local Enterprise Partnerships (LEPs) emerged. However, in late 2011 the board of the association decided to cease operations from the end of March 2012, since several members felt that they wished to concentrate on LEP areas and that cross-boundary policy dimensions were insufficient to warrant the continuance of the association. As a result of the success described above, it was recognised that there continued to be a significant north-west aspect to European structural funding and the north-west Universities European Unit was 'spun out' to continue to support members on this.

While sub-national arrangements are now in a new phase, the demand for inter-university collaboration and greater university impact has increased, not diminished. This chapter prompts the question as to where both the catalyst and the mechanisms to facilitate this beyond LEP boundaries will come from in the absence of NWUA. This challenge is often compounded by reductions in the levels of expertise and experience arising from the natural staff movement and wastage across universities resulting from financial pressures. It is not within the authors' remit to provide an answer. However, the real and lasting achievements of NWUA show what can be achieved by universities working together in a favourable policy context.

NOTE

1. Including Learning and Teaching, Research, Enterprise, Cultural and Creative Industries, Health and Social Care, Skills and Widening Participation.

CONCLUSION

The Regional Role of the University

Patrick Diamond

This book provides a systematic overview of the strategic role of the modern university in regional economic and social development throughout the advanced economy nations. Most of the case studies draw on experience in the United Kingdom, but several authors range wider to consider developments in other industrialised and developing nations. The unifying theme of the collection is that higher education institutions are not only sites for the development and transfusion of knowledge, but are at the centre of developments in the emergence of the post-industrial economy and society.

There have been disagreements going back many centuries about the purpose of the university: in contemporary times, neoliberal narratives in the United States and Britain have emphasised the contribution of higher education to national economic efficiency, productivity, and wealth creation. However, dissenters argue that universities are not just about economic growth: institutions of higher learning underpin a common culture of social critique, humanitarian values, and respect for democracy. It is argued that universities have become too skewed towards narrow economic imperatives. As the cultural theorist Terry Eagleton has reflected:

> We have witnessed in our own time the death of universities as centres of critique... The role of academia has been to service the status quo, not challenge it in the name of justice, tradition, imagination, human welfare, the free play of the mind or alternative visions of the future. We will not change this simply by increasing state funding of the humanities as opposed to slashing it to nothing. We will change it by insisting that a critical reflection on human values and principles should be central to everything that goes on in universities, not just to the study of Rembrandt or Rimbaud.[1]

Yet it is surely possible to balance the role of universities as engines of growth with their function as centres of social research and criticism. The authors in this volume address a wide variety of issues and themes, but arguably four key arguments stand out throughout the book.

The first is that universities are set to play a crucial role in the aftermath of the UK's decision to leave the European Union (EU). Although Britain is leaving the EU, its connections to continental Europe and the wider world are likely to remain of vital importance. The role that universities play in bridging the UK with global hubs of information and knowledge is likely to be even more crucial in the wake of Britain's departure from the EU.

The second argument of the book is that higher education institutions remain a critical agent of growth and innovation in underperforming regions of the UK economy, with or without Brexit. Universities are part of what is termed 'the triple helix' of government, higher education and the private sector as a dynamic lever of growth. The British economy has been increasingly centred on knowledge production rather than physical production, further emphasising the importance of higher education research and innovation. Regions without a high quality HEI risk falling further behind in the race for national and international competitiveness. Tackling regional inequalities also requires long-term investment in infrastructure and productive assets through new approaches to financing public services. It requires world-class health and education, accompanied by investment in skills, science, knowledge and innovation.

The great economist J.M. Keynes foresaw even in the 1920s that the debate about the role of public institutions such as universities concerns the 'agenda' and 'non-agenda' of government[2]. The argument was that the state should do only what is not being done adequately already by markets. However, it is increasingly clear that market failure extends well beyond conventional areas of supply-side intervention in the economy, such as skills, science and research. A short-term business culture in Britain has prevented firms from nurturing new products and services. Why does so much technological innovation originate in Britain, but so few start-ups grow into world-beating high-tech companies? Too few small and medium-sized enterprises can access finance for growth. Why does Britain have fewer micro-businesses than any comparable industrial economy? Despite its financial services sophistication, why does the City seem incapable of channelling savings into long-term projects that enhance Britain's productive potential beyond London and the south-east? Too few sectors are actively championed as beacons of national success. Why do French, German and Scandinavian governments celebrate national companies, but British governments generally do not? To make an impact on economic performance, universities have to be able to work alongside a genuinely enabling state.

The third argument of the volume is that universities can make a major social impact, not only an economic impact. Higher education institutions use their knowledge in order to improve society: from ensuring better health care treatment to improving the quality of life in local communities and neighbourhoods. Universities are 'anchor institutions' that can help to strengthen the sense of belonging and place, while helping to deliver world-class public services. Public services are currently facing multiple challenges in relation to how they are financed, organised and run: demographic change is increasing the structural pressures on public services. New technologies can help to solve problems, but also lead to rising costs.

The downside for individuals in a dynamic, innovating economy is that the rapidity of technological change threatens incumbent companies, making skills redundant and destroying jobs in ways no one can presently foresee. Just as the NHS was founded on the principle that no one can have perfect knowledge of whether they will enjoy good health in the future, and therefore collective insurance is the most equitable solution, social security needs to be re-thought for an age of ever more rapid economic change, as individuals seek more choice around how to balance work and family life. HEIs will play a critical role in helping to design more effective and cost-efficient public services, while constructing a system of social security that equips people adequately for a world of rapid change.

Finally, the authors in the book argue that regional universities are part of a global network of information and knowledge beyond the purview of any single nation state. This has profound implications for the future of public governance, since universities operate at multiple levels of decision-making: local, regional, national, and international. Increasingly, HEIs need to be able to take account of these multiple perspectives and decision points in all that they do.

In summary, the risk of globalisation over the last three decades has been that it will amplify the gaps between the 'winners' and 'losers' of change, creating a permanently marginalised minority with little stake in the nation's future. The aim of universities working alongside government and the private sector must be to create balanced and sustainable economic growth to improve the living standards of the whole of the population, ensuring that Britain grows together rather than apart. That requires genuine partnership between the public and private sector where the state invests proactively in economic potential. However, this collection of essays attests that HEIs have an essential role to play in society beyond economic growth, in particular to address the condition of Britain and its communities that is not confined to any particular measure of GDP. World-class universities make a vital contribution towards our quality of life and common culture.

NOTES

1. Eagleton Terry "The death of universities" The Guardian Dec 17, 2010 Available at: https://www.theguardian.com/commentisfree/2010/dec/17/death-universities-malaise-tuition-fees [Last accessed: 09/01/18].

2. Keynes J. M. The End of Laissez-Faire. In: Essays in Persuasion. Palgrave Macmillan, London, 2010.